Rome T

I0172028

What if Rome never fell!

It seemed such a small thing when Julius Caesar discovered the bicycle, but his acute mind instantly saw how this was the great game changer. Armies could get to battle many times faster and not be exhausted when they got there, communication took on new dimensions, so many advantages.

With this single invention, so much changes. Caesar survives (Because he has a bike to escape the assassins) and Rome never falls, and continues spreading its empire across the world to the present day!

Yet the republic is a victim of it's own success. 2000 years on, and not a lot has changed — Until a little known troupe of un-funny comedians called Eruptus Non-Funnius decide they are heartily sick of sacrificing chickens.

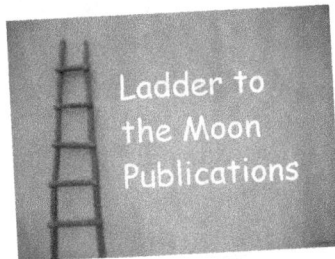

Ladder to the Moon Publications

"The man who is tenacious of purpose in a rightful cause is not shaken from his firm resolve by the frenzy of his fellow citizens clamoring for what is wrong, or by the tyrant's threatening countenance."

Horace

Rome Too

COPYRIGHT 2020   Ecallaw Leachim
This book is published under the Berne Convention. All copyright protected to the author. No prior use without permission except for excerpts for review or educational purposes. All enquiries via Email to:
info.numberharmonics@gmail.com
Published by Ladder to the Moon Publications.
ISBN 978-0-6484277-1-1

*"Mingle a little folly with your wisdom:
A little nonsense now and then is pleasant."*

Horace

Dedicated to Geoffrey John Wallace

Rome Too is a tribute to the extraordinary humour and wit
of my father, Geoffrey John Wallace. Giving someone life
is one thing, giving them an appreciation of it is
another thing entirely.

Other Books by this Author:

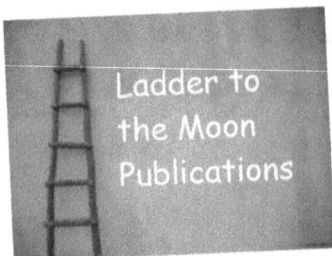

INDEX

Sliced bread! Brilliant Idea, but what can I DO with it?

Out, out, brief candle!
Life's but a walking shadow,
A poor player that struts and frets his hour
upon the stage, and then is heard no more:
it is a tale told by an idiot,
full of sound and fury, signifying nothing.

Macbeth (c. 1605), Act V, Scene 5, line 23.

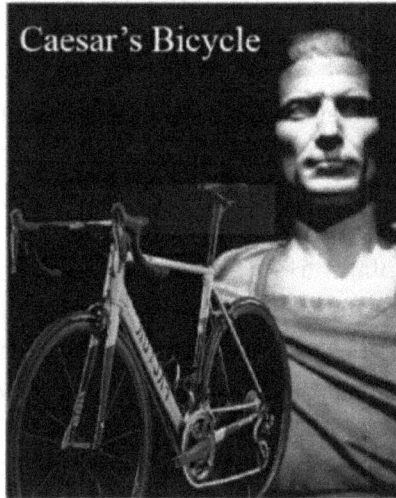

Caesar's Bicycle

Introduction

Who would have thought how such a simple invention as the bicycle would change the known world. Because of this tool, Caesar and his armies could get everywhere so much quicker. The fabulous Roman Roads meant he was now able to contain the barbarians and defend the Empire far more effectively.

Obviously, when the famous assassination attempt came along, he used his new bicycle and was able to hop onto it and ride away. Thus the Republic survived, democracy continued, there was no civil war and with the continuing peace, the Fall of Rome never happened.

His chosen adopted son, Augustus, attained the President's chair (another unique Caesarean invention - an elected chief) and the Caesarian bloodline held sway for a thousand years.

As a result, there was no dark age, no rise of Christianity to a state religion, no arguments with Muslims over Jerusalem (because it never left Roman hands) no world wars, no Hitler and no oil shortage.

Obviously, oil was important, but it was Olive Oil that everyone argued over. Yes, there were disputes over land and arguments over inheritance, but overall the Roman Empire was a stable and prosperous place where culture and arts flourished.

Until that fateful day when Eruptus Non Funnius, a troupe of unfunny comedians, decided NOT to sacrifice a chicken!

Of course, there had always been tides of change but, as Roman Law had held sway for so long, there had been no need for a Magna Carta, nor a reformation or even a renaissance. Leo Vinci was still a popular classical author and his funny stories about chasing the Moaning Lisa were now considered standard texts for study.

Naturally, statue-making was, as it will always be, the favourite pursuit of the rich. Not that they slaved over hard stone for months themselves, they were rich, as I explained! All the best houses had shadow sculptors working in the background. They created "stone selfies" - usually a bust with a big smile full of perfect teeth, and always carved in white marble.

Sadly, there were still Americans. They were known, of course, for their bad Latin, and north of where they lived there were Canadians, known for their bad Gaulish but, apart from these small blips, things proceeded along rather smoothly.

Then, everything changed. From out the blue, a troupe of up-and-coming un-funny comedians decided to leave the old country and put on a new show at the Coliseum recently erected in New Rome. So our story starts in America, the land of the rich and home to innumerable examples of terrible fashion sense.

I give you fair warning! For those who like the old ways, the sudden alteration to norms this book offers will have some asking, 'Why in the name of Hades did they deviate from the simple things, like tossing Christians into the maws of beasts?' (I am assured by the lions they taste quite good) The simple answer was that people were bored. They wanted a change.

When asked how it all happened years later, the famous historian, Butcherous Wordicus, shrugged his shoulders and explained the sudden onset of newness in terms everyone pretended to understand.

He went, "Meh!"

Or, as Rufus Maximus, the gallant leader of the small cadre of un-funny comedians known as Eruptus Non-Funnius said to his troupe back before where it all started. "We need something fresh, something that will really get them going!" From that tiny seed, from that one person deciding they needed a point of difference, this entire sorry saga evolved.

It all started one day on the ox-drawn train to central New Rome.

The Suit

Acting like he knew something, the Patrician strutted into their carriage. Claudius Hemus Spectre was a gaunt, unsmiling creature. He had the classical Roman appearance: long, straight nose, blue eyes, blonde hair, stiff formal posture - however, there was one thing about him was quite different: He didn't wear a Toga.

Claudius was dressed in the latest fashion, the suit. A sharp grey pinstripe number, three-piece with a silk tie that shone with a sort of orange glare - one that could harm rabbits at twenty paces. He strolled in to meet his new charges with the aplomb of a person knowing they were at the peak of fashion, yet also understanding that not one of these plebs before him could possibly understand this.

Rufus Maximus was 'one of those plebs'. He was the very bottom of the barrel and proud of it. Raised in the slums of Old Rome by his prostitute mother, whose only notable quality was that every hour of every day, she would curse the father he had never seen for going off and getting himself killed in some war. (Rufus always suspected she was covering up the fact she had no idea who his father was.)

As the Ox Train rattled along, his doleful eyes (so used to assessing every new situation for threat) looked up at the Patrician. The man seemed calibrated for witty retorts, and little else. The greatest risk he saw coming from the fellow was an almost complete lack of enthusiasm for anything, and most especially them. Rufus sighed. His troupe was tired, coming from over the Atlantic and Rome (which you 'could' refer to as Old Rome if you wished) only days before.

A storm had sent them North of New Rome, thus the Ox Cart Train from Bostonium to New Rome. The prospect of lucrative work offered by the employer of this strange creature before them had coaxed him from the secure poverty of the old country to try their luck in New Rome.

They stood there, eyeing each other off for a few minutes. All the strange styles of dress the Americans wore were a never-ending source of fascination for him, but Rufus said nothing. Before him was a meal ticket and, however absurd its appearance might be, he initially felt obliged to not bite the hand that would potentially be feeding them.

This impulse died soon after the Patrician started talking.

Claudius noted Rufus, reasonably intelligent, badly dressed, not much of a hygiene buff by the smell of him. He had dour blue eyes, a hook nose, and skin that looked like it had been used by bacteria to play blackheads on. His hair was uncombed, as was the way with travelling unfunny comedians, and between the oily snatches a hint of baldness was starting to show. The fellow still had all his teeth, surprisingly.

Claudius then looked over to the other fellow, whom he guessed to be Ofal, the second member of the troupe. He was one of those extraordinarily unexceptional people to look at. When you think of 'middle of the road' you naturally think of road kill, and this was close to the depth of presence you got from the fellow - And just like road kill, his smell reminded you he was there.

The only one that seemed vaguely interesting was the girl, Meridius. This could have been entirely due to the fact she was a girl, of course. She was pretty - sort of. She was intelligent - sort of. She had terrible dress sense, that was certain. The clothes seemed more like rags that had leapt onto her for a free ride, but the hair was the complete shocker. It sprouted out in a mad array that gave her that distinctly fashionable look of being stark raving bonkers.

"What do you call it?" Rufus asked the Patrician who had been sent out as their agent.

"What do I call what?" Claudius shot back, looking at the fellow in much the same way a cat looks at a mangy street dog.

"The thingy stuff, the clothes. What do you call it?"

"Oh, the latest fashion? It is a suit."

"Who does it suit?"

"Me, I am in a suit."

"You are suing someone? Worse, you are suing ME?"

"No, what I am wearing is CALLED a suit. Are you stupid?"

"I am not the one wearing the suit." Rufus sniffed back indignantly.

The mutual dislike between the two was immediate, but Meridius, the one girl-clown of the troupe saved the moment by pointing out the window of their carriage, saying, "Look, a new statue to Caesar!"

Ofal Biggins, a man known more for his jowls than his good looks, snorted. "Another one? Why can't the Patricians find some imagination and carve someone other than themselves, Caesar or Augustus? And on that subject, why isn't there a month for Caesar?"

Rufus snapped back, "Idiot, what do you think July is for?"

Meridius ignored them and said in a soft voice, because she loved Caesar, "Oh look, and they have him on his bicycle as well!"

Ofal snorted, "On his bike, like every other damn statue to Caesar. How original."

"No, this is different," Meridius responds with enormous enthusiasm. "Because they have updated him to a geared model. That is really exciting stuff, a total break from tradition. I love New Rome, it is cutting edge."

"Like the suit!" exclaimed Claudius.

She looked him up and down, shielding her eyes from the tie. "Is the orange thing around your neck a sort of emergency suicide aid?" she asked.

Claudius laughed at her provincial innocence. "No darling, it is a phallic symbol."

Rufus sneered openly. "If I had a phallus like that I would commit suicide."

Claudius could see where this was going, and took a broad-sweep view to salvage the situation. "Look people, you have come a long way, all expenses paid, to do a tour of the new countries, starting here in New Rome. I am your agent and unless we all want to have a miserable time, we need to set aside opinions and snide little comments (he looked accusingly at Rufus) and get on. Agreed?"

"All expenses paid!" Rufus laughed. "We had to sit in the slaves galley and help row the damn boat!"

Claudius made no apology. "You know how it is, all hands on deck, or below deck as the case may be. The thing is, you are here. You didn't die or get scurvy, so I expect a little gratitude for all we have done for you. This is an opportunity, people!"

All of them instinctively reached to their necks to touch the little statue of OPS hiding there in a leather bag. Then, for good measure, they fondle the other one, Lucre, as well.

"Bless the Lord Ops," said Rufus and the others in unison.

"That's more like it. Gratitude goes a long way in this town, and respect. As you know, I am Patrician class and can get you people in doors where otherwise, if you tried to walk through, you would be laughed at. In fact, they would kick you out and throw the slops bucket over you to boot. I believe I deserve a little gratitude as I am going out of my way to help you, if you please."

Claudius stood up in his Patrician stance, much like a show dog when it is being judged.

"So kind of you, Patrician, to lower yourself to cater to we mere plebs," Rufus said, sarcastically. "It makes me wonder just how poor you must be to do this job, which is to say, very?"

Claudius cut him a withering squint. In his own circle, this would suffice to silence his equals, but here, all it did was make Rufus laugh.

Meridius saved the day. "We thank you, Patrician, for going out of your way to help we mere plebs."

"That's more like it, my pleasure," Claudius responded, pretending he didn't hear what might well have been sarcasm. "What I need to know right now is the prece' to the show, so I can discuss things with the stage manager at the Coliseum. Did you prepare an outline?"

Rufus settled down. Well, this is why they were here, to start the next wave in the new countries. "Only one significant change from the standard performance stuff - no sacrifice to the Gods," he said.

Claudius did a classic double-take.

"What!" he spluttered. "Are you mad? You cannot flagrantly go against tradition like that! The crowd will crucify you!"

They had been through it a hundred times, and yes, they did have to run from crucifixion a good number of times, this was true. "Eruptus Non-Funnius are not the usual run-of-the-mill unfunny comedians. We have principles in this troupe. One of the principles is that all these sacrificial animals cost a lot of money we don't have. Now, by all means, throw a Christian to the lions if you must before we go on, but no gutting of sheep, or chickens, or goats, and reading of the entrails. We just do not believe in that superstitious nonsense."

"You people are insane." Claudius shook his head. "You are going directly against more than two thousand years of tradition. Why do you think we throw Christians to the lions? Yes, I know the ritual cannibalism is bad, but the truth is, they are lion food specifically because they do not sacrifice! Worse, they got all these farmers agreeing with them, saying they are Christians, and stating religious differences as a legal excuse to withhold their oxen when the cart came round to collect their animals for whatever ritual was about to happen.

"You KNOW what happens after that - lion feeding! Why are you deliberately trying to provoke alarm?" Claudius was deeply shocked. He really didn't care if this lot got fed to lions, but as their manager, he might be tarred with the same brush. Did his boss know this was happening?

"And how did you get this act cleared in the old country? How can you all still be alive?"

"We did mostly country work," Ofal explained. "Honestly, the farmers were relieved when they could take their chickens back home. They even asked if we were secret Christians because ALL of them were. You would be surprised how many there are, despite all the lions being fed."

"My dear Plebs," Claudius explained. "This is New Rome. This is a NEW coliseum. People are GOING to expect sacrifices because they need to know if the omens are good. It is not a complicated thing, spill the entrails, get an augur to read the signs, but be sure to pay him enough to ensure the signs are good. Otherwise, we are all on dangerous ground."

Meridius chirped up. "Did you know, a lot of cities we performed in, the people were relieved they didn't have to sit through yet another sacrifice. It really is a waste of time and all we are doing is entertainment, after all. Do we REALLY need to know if the sky is going to fall during this performance?" Then she is distracted and looking out the window says, "Oh look, another statue of Caesar on a bicycle!"

"Attention span of a goldfish," Rufus explained to Claudius as Meridius sat there waving to Caesar. "But it is true, we have had precious few complaints from the people, they don't mind at all. It is always management that BELIEVES it is important."

"Of course they do!" exclaimed Claudius. "The plebs go home to their hovels, they have nothing to lose. But if you start bringing bad luck to any establishment by not performing the required religious rites, they stand to lose quite a lot. What happens when they get audited and asked to prove the number of sacrifices performed? Three days in the Tarquin and a big fine for every missed sacrifice. And WHY? Because NO ONE wants bad luck to fall on their heads."

Rufus snorted. "It is such circular logic. If you don't perform a sacrifice, you go to jail for three days, and it costs you, which therefore proves it is bad luck. Honestly, the whole thing is just too ridiculous and the State needs to wake up and smell the roses."

Claudius laughed at the naiveté, "The State does not care what you or I think. It says a sacrifice must be made, so a sacrifice WILL be made. No sacrifice equals no performance, and otherwise, sorry you came all this way for nothing."

Meridius has a light bulb moment. "I have a solution, guys! What we can do is a RITUAL ritual sacrifice. What we do is use a RUBBER chicken, with RUBBER entrails! We have one in the props and so we CAN perform the ritual the State requires - yet still make our point!"

Rufus looked up at her. Surprisingly, this made sense. He looks over to Claudius, "Does the State specifically say a LIVING chicken is to be sacrificed?"

Claudius is aghast. "Everyone knows they mean a living chicken. The rules don't specifically say this exactly, but everyone knows you can't read rubber damn entrails and get a good augury."

"Well, the law only says a sacrifice must be made before each performance and it nominates as a suitable animal for common or ordinary sacrificial rituals that you use a chicken, sheep, goat or pig, yes? However, it doesn't say you CAN'T sacrifice a dog, or a butterfly, or an iguana, just as it doesn't specifically state you can't sacrifice a rubber chicken." Rufus laid out his case.

"Of course you cannot sacrifice a rubber chicken! It's not alive to be sacrificed!" Claudius shouts.

"Precisely, which is why this is a RITUAL ritual sacrifice," Rufus exclaimed, not quite understanding why this fellow cannot see the obvious. "Seriously, this is even better than no sacrifice at all. Think of all the free publicity we will get!"

"Look," says Meridius, "A statue of Caesar actually ON his bicycle. Oh, that is just beautiful."

Claudius shook his head, and sat down in a rather stunned confusion. His mind was racing around the ramifications of how this would play out, and how much of a beating the boss was going to give him as a result.

Silence ensued between all parties as the rattle of wooden wheels rumbled on the tracks taking this one small group of individuals to their date with destiny.

Humour is often stronger and more effective than sharpness in cutting knotty issues.

Horace

After the Show

The performance brought boos, jeers with many things being thrown at the small troupe. A suitable response was subsequently made by Rufus, standing there, insulting the crowd by suggesting what their mothers must have done with dogs for them to exist. This cause further uproar and shouting. It was going BRILLIANTLY, plus they scored a big razoo from the resident Priest, standing in for Jupiter as he did. The old fellow seemed utterly incensed! In all, an enormously successful show.

"Well, what did I say? The rubber chicken really worked a treat and got them booing and stamping feet right from the start. Brilliant move Meridius darling!" said Rufus as they ran from the Green Room with their props.

"They really want blood, don't they," noted Ofal. "We prepped them good for the Gladiators. That rubber chicken sent the audience crazy. It is a keeper. I loved the reaction from the Augury though, how much did you pay him for that?"

Meridius was busy stopping to admire a statue of Caesar with Augustus, standing next to their bikes and Rufus had to drag her away. "Come on dear, no slacking. You never know what sort of vengeful twat will be after us. Mustn't hang about. And no, Ofal, I paid no one. Do you think we have that sort of money, to splash cash around like that?"

"It was a fairly extreme reaction, don't you think?" Ofal commented as, out of breath, he threw the stage kit into the back of their donkey cart.

"Really? I didn't notice. I was focussed on my lines."

Meridius was now looking up at the moon, talking to it in a strange tongue. Neither of the men paid much attention to her, other than shake their heads and lift her up onto the donkey as they made their get-a-way.

Ofal said, "Well, when you did the 'This is my Chicken, my genuine artificial chicken, and these are the entrails, the absolutely genuinely unreal entrails!' the audience looked kind of perplexed. But when you pricked your finger over the rubber entrails and said, in very good Latin I must add, 'hoc enim est sanguis pullum.' I really don't think they got the idea that a drop of your blood was representing the chicken's blood.

"If you had said ' hoc verum est sanguis. efficit vitam pullum.' explaining that the blood was real and that it only REPRESENTED the chicken, they may have grasped the concept better. But regardless, the Augur really went off after that. He came up, inspected the entrails, screamed, then ran off, shouting the Roman Empire was doomed." Ofal explained.

"Did he now?" Rufus asked with curiosity. "A bit of an extreme reaction over a fake ritual. Do you think he took it all seriously?"

"Indubitably so," responded Ofal, exercising his 'big' word for the week. "But now I think of it, because he did have such a big reaction, maybe the ritual actually worked?"

"I hope not," replied Rufus with concern. "It would be bad for business if Rome collapsed. The barbarians have no appreciation of theatre at all."

A growing noise in the background told them what they needed to hear - It seemed that the Rubber Chicken had done it's job and Eruptus Non-Funnius were suddenly a big hit. As in - Lots of people wanted to hit them, which meant (if they managed to get away without being crucified) that very soon they would be in significant demand.

"I agree that the rubber chicken stays IN!" declared Rufus. "I reckon it going to be the next big thing."

With the cart loaded and all insignia of the troupe removed from the sides, they made their way past the crowds that had gathered outside to beat up the comedians. A fellow saw them and called out, "Have you seen the actors with the Rubber Chicken?"

Dressed as they now were with hoods and cloaks over their acting outfits, and given the extremely low IQ of the Plebs that went to see their shows, Rufus felt secure in answering, "Yes, they went THAT way!"

Why they fall for it, he will never know, but the mob took the heavy wooden cross they had just knocked up from bleacher planks and went raging away in the direction he indicated.

Rolling out into the streets of New Rome, they got to do a little sight seeing. In the background, a street vendor is wheeling about on a bike, dressed like Caesar, calling out, "Sliced bread, get your sliced bread here! Get your sliced bread!" Rufus just shook his head, astounded with all the new inventions.

"I tell you Ofal, New Rome is just full of bright new innovations. Imagine, pre-sliced bread! That will really shake the dross out of the conservatives. That is the best idea since non-sliced bread!" Rufus goes over to buy some of this fabulous and inventive concept and casually asked the vendor what you DO with this new and unique invention.

Still shouting, the man explains, "You take TWO slices, one in either hand, and you put a sausage on it and a bit of sauce, then put them together and eat!"

"I don't get it," Rufus says, confused. "If I am holding two slices in either hand, how do I pick up the sausage to put in on there?"

"Exactly Sir - a difficult and tricky operation, which is why you get your slave to do it."

"But I don't have a slave," Rufus explained.

"Poverty DOES make it difficult for you to make the most of this new invention," the street vendor shakes his head sadly. Then he has an idea, "Do you have anyone who can help out?"

"Well, yes, I do."

"Fine, well THEY can hold the slices of bread, while YOU put on the sausage and the sauce."

"Brilliant idea!" said Rufus. "I will take some!"

oooo000000oooo

Back in the Coliseum, Claudius was still standing there, rubbing his chin. Not because he was thinking, but because some yobbo had swung at him and it hurt. He sat back down to contemplate these recent events.

It was a weird performance - very weird - but it got a big reaction. The rubber chicken thing was so strange, yet it worked! The people were already crying for blood and just went crazy when the Gladiators finally came out. It was a shocking bending of the rules to get a cheap insult, but it did the job.

He got out his wax tablet and made notes for the boss. The Augury though, that was really odd. Calling out about the Empire being doomed and all ... He wondered how the actors got the money to pay for such a great performance. Etruscans like that guy were never cheap.

They were all still booing and jeering when he left the stands to head home. Flagging down a passing cart, he hopped in and gave his address. "Bronxinium" he says, already knowing how it will be taken.

You know you have to move to better digs when even the ox-cart driver looks down their nose at your address. Maybe, just maybe, this strange troupe of unknown actors was his meal ticket out of the extreme poverty his patrician self was so allergic to.

"Make money, money by fair means if you can,
if not, but any means money."
Horace

Tracking Down the Story

The little show by the unknown and unimportant actor troupe known as Eruptus-Non-Funnius would have normally passed by without too much scrutiny, but a reporter by the name of Garam Marsala just happened to be there for the opening and was genuinely shocked at the use of a fake ritual ritual.

Of itself, no big thing, but he worked for the New Rome Times, in the employ of Lord Rupus Murdochius, that ruthless seeker of any type of truth he can manipulate, massage or masticate into something he can sell.

Garam was also surprised at the reaction of the Augury. Clearly, the man had been paid to fake it. So he noted this on the lists and made a recommendation that the fellow should go up the Tarquin for a bit. Not for the bribe, which you expect as normal business practice, but for the terrible overacting. End of Rome? - by the GODS, what a cheap way to stir up the crowd.

He got back to file his report, yet when he looked up the name of the Etruscan on for the night he was shocked to learn it was the LEAD Augury. Passably strange. Maybe this needed looking into?

Well, being a reporter he got onto it right away and ordered pizza. It is a little known fact that Pizza - possibly because it was so difficult to digest - keeps you up at night so you can really think things through. "Make sure you get them to douse it with Garum and Parmesan. I don't want my nose able to smell anything but rotten fish and vomit when eating my pizza," he said to his slave as he sent him down to the local. "And don't forget the beer!" he shouted as an afterthought.

Then he sat back to consider things. As everyone knows, the secret to writing a good story is the headline. If you want to sell a papyrus, it has to have a catchy title. It also needs an interview! He clapped his hands and his former lawyer who had fallen onto hard times and was now his slave, Chincino, appeared at the door.

"Yes Master," he said bowing. What he doesn't say is "I see your dress sense hasn't improved." or "That belly has eaten one too many pizzas, you know." Chincino learned very quickly that the passing conversation you might have had as a free man changed markedly once you fell into slave status.

Still, Garam Marsala was not the worst of masters, just stupid - which for a smart slave was a positive boon. His plain and un-romanly round face was unmarked by the remnants of pox, as clear a sign of Patrician heritage as any, because your mother kept you off the streets and made you learn Latin. Which in turn led the dear man into his position with the New Rome Times.

The faded Toga, lack of rouge and general slack jowled disinterest in life were the clearest indicators of a Patrician on the rag heap, as they would say. But this was the very reason he chose Garam as a Master. He was not important enough to be particularly cruel, not wise enough to realise he was being shepherded along like a puppet. In all, an acceptable balance until Chincino could find a doorway to an improved lifestyle.

"Got to get a good story. I want you to find and organise a meeting with the Head Augury of New Rome, the Etruscan fellow. Focus Maximus is his name. I need a quote or three from him to put into an article I am working on. As everyone knows, astonishingly biased interviews are necessary if you are to successfully convert your fanciful notions into a form that gives them meaning and portent."

"You mean you need to concoct a good story to please your master?" Chincino suggested, dryly.

Garam looked up at his smart-ass slave. He really should whip him, but essentially, the fellow was right. Lord Rupus pretty much owned his staff. But other than the lip, his former solicitor was a competent slave.

Chincino was a Greek and, as mentioned, Garam's erstwhile solicitor. He had gotten himself into financial trouble and offered to sell himself into slavery if Garam could cover the debt. Garam generously offered to sort out his bills, not with cash, of course. Patricians have no money, but plenty of guile. The reporter managed to pay Chincino's debt by threatening to write a series of articles on the mob boss who owned the debt. Nothing like blackmail to get a free slave, Garam said to himself, smugly, and without any hint of dichotomy at the notion of a 'free slave'.

"Just find the augury. He made a crazy prediction and I need to know more about it." Garam said.

With Chincino off to get the Etruscan, Garam settled down to go over the sorts of omens he would need to back up the report. First, what important signs did he see when travelling there? Maybe that dog sexing another dog? No, far too common. Maybe the rat staring at him from a window ledge? Again, far too common. The orphan child weeping in the street? Very common, but it might work. It was indicative of loneliness, being bereft, etc. That would do, so he got to writing up his preliminary.

"Foul FOWL! (Not a bad headline) Insane Head Augury of New Rome in hoax ritual using Rubber Chicken. Swears it will end civilisation as we know it! Lonely orphan child seen weeping in the stree ts backs up prediction. And what caused this furore? Actors from the Old Country stirred up the crowd and had the mob calling for real blood after fake

sacrifice was performed. Senator Praxlis was in the audience. He called Eruptus Non-Funnius, the troupe of unfunny comedians in question, 'Extremely funny, and by funny I mean strange!' More news as it comes to hand!"

Garam sent the wax table to his secretary to set the contents on papyrus, then smiled broadly as his pizza and beer arrived. An hour later with the prece' done, he sent it off by pigeon to Lord Rupus. The was confident the boss would like it, which translated to the piece being likely to sell some papyrus!

Happy and with a full belly, he headed off to bed for some shut-eye. He rather liked the story so far. It would be something to tickle the people's interest in the morning press, which means it sells, which means Lord Rupus will be happy and all this means is that he will still have a job.

Blissfully falling into dreams, Garam Masala had absolutely no idea of the depth and size of the avalanche he had just released At that point in time, the fellow generally believed that, as a journalistic hack, he was merely throwing off yet another pointless meandering regarding the day to day events of New Rome.

Come the morrow, he would see things very differently.

The next morning was the start of it all. "Did you track down the Augury?" Garam asked Chincino.

"Yes, but he's taken a vow of silence." answered his slave.

"So, will he speak to me, then?"

"No, he's taken a vow of silence."

"He can't be too damn silent if he told you he was taking a vow of silence," Garam noted the obvious.

"He told me in sign language," Chincino replied.

"Well, really. That's a bit of a give-a-way, isn't it? You have to doubt the integrity of an Augury who takes a vow of silence yet still 'speaks' in sign language. But maybe you got it wrong, it wasn't a VOW he had taken, it was just a few silent VOWELS?"

Chincino was a good and obedient slave, who correctly considered his owner an idiot. "Just what I was thinking, boss," (he wasn't thinking this at all) "But be this as it may be, he's not talking to anyone."

"Take me to him and bring me the big stick." Garam was smiling with menace as he explained to his slave. "So many people who take vows of silence reverse that decision when they see the big stick."

Chincino did so, and when bringing it back, asked, "Why does your bat had the words 'The Fifth' inscribed into it? Garam smiled,

"I call it 'The Fifth' because when someone tells me they want to take 'The Fifth' I make sure I give them ALL their rights, and a few lefts as well."

It took an hour to donkey over to the Soothsayers hovel (Why do they always live in hovels?) and Garam was feeling his big stick the whole way. He had nothing against auguries, despite the fact that most of them were Etruscan, but withholding news from a State-sanctioned reporter such as himself was a crime. But rather than go through courts, bribe judges, pay off the bailiffs, etc. it was simply easier to beat the information out of them.

The curious nature of Roman Law was that it was reserved for Romans. Which made perfect sense! If it was fair and just for everyone, then it would be called 'everyones' law, wouldn't it? Now, the vast majority of soothsayers were, in fact, Roman, but to command better money you had to be Etruscan. So, by and large, they all claimed this nationality, thus leaving themselves open to beatings should they be so foolish as to take vows of silence.

Walking through the low door, Garam noticed two things. First, the lack of furniture. Second, the lack of people. His razor-sharp mind quickly calculated the possibilities and he came to the conclusion, "We are at the wrong house, idiot!" and he hits Chincino over the head with the stick.

"I was just thinking that myself," says Chincino, rubbing his head. "But there IS another alternative, Master Garam. Perhaps, being an Augury, he foresaw what would happen and took off?"

"Fuddlebugs," said Garam, recognising the obvious. "You could be right. Let's catch a donkey to the city militia and report an absconding soothsayer."

Chincino looked down and, in the dust, he saw a note. He picked it up, it read, "The end of Rome is upon us! I am going to throw myself off the Tarquin! See you all in Hades." It was signed with the head augury's seal, so no question it was him. "Ah, Boss - something you might want to see!"

"Right after we get the matter reported, Chincino. This is a serious business and we need to inform the authorities right away."

Oooo000000oooo

"The HEAD augury, you say?" the retired army Sergent words had the right sort of cynicism to them to tell you how he didn't think this was particularly important. He also looked like he did not have much by way of brainpower.

"Yes, yes - the HEAD augury." Garam was impatiently tapping the counter. The whole morning had been wasted on this. He turned to Chincino and asked, "What was the fellows name?"

"Focus Maximus," he said, ducking a swipe from the Sergent as he spoke.

"Slaves need to ask permission to speak!" the policeman said, gruffly, very annoyed that the pecking order had been ignored. "So, what did you say his name was?" He looked at Chincino with a raised eyebrow, daring the slave to speak again. Chincino was no fool and kept his mouth shut.

"Focus Maximus it is then," said the Sergent. Taking out some wax tablets, lifting his stylus in the air, and generally acting as if he was about to start getting down the details. But he paused, and looked up for the next all-important question. "Oh, by the way, are you Patrician or Pleb?" he asked the reporter.

"Working Patrician," Garam sighed, hating the fact that he represented the lowest rung on the social ladder - the working Patrician. The Militia Sergent just smiled, they both knew if he said "Pleb" the forms went back under the counter and he was told to come back next month, due to the extensive waiting list.

There was almost no waiting list, of course. Sorting crime in New Rome was largely rounding up drunk gamblers in the early hours or beating up beggars. But there WAS a pecking order, which was largely decided by either your station or your bribes, and usually by a bit of both.

Of course, New Rome was not perfect. There were assassinations, wife beatings, and obviously bribes, but these things were not a crime. They were essentially civil misdemeanors that were handled by the Tribune of the Plebs. But for actual crimes, you needed the police, who were all retired army veterans.

Unfortunately, while their rates of bribery were very reasonable, albeit depending on the class of person to be dealt with, they also tended to be very slow. Indeed, things were not moving along as quickly as Garam had hoped. He sighed, being a member of the Patrician class was not what it used to be. After a few thousand years of breeding, there was not only an awful lot of them but, with the division of inheritance the vast majority, such as Garam, were rather poor. Patrician by name, yet essentially working class.

Yes, he was well above the policeman in social circles, but it made little difference. These ex-vets were just not jumping to attention like they used to in the old days.

The greatest advantage to Patrician blood was, however, the fact you COULD get a decent job. More to the point, the decent jobs went first to

Patricians and, as there were so many of them, it meant the truly crap jobs were the only ones left for the others. As slaves generally did those, the employment opportunities for plebs were essentially non-existent unless you got into the public service or took up blacksmithing.

Yes, you 'could' get work mucking out stalls and cleaning the streets, but as this was usually done by the slaves, the rate of pay was insignificant. As a result, most of the people you would consider as lower-class Romans were essentially unemployed lay-a-bouts or ex-vets.

Most of these former military men were out in the country, but if they lived in town they were invariably policeman. And, as policeman, they had a job for life, which meant they had absolutely no interest in helping working-class patricians like Garam Marsala who came in with complaints.

The Sergent subsequently looked up over the counter to the fellows slave, and asked, "Can you write?" Chincino, wise enough to say nothing, simply nodded in the affirmative. "Good, you can take down the details, then." The Sergent nodded as if the matter was dealt with and went back to his friends to continue his dice game from where they had left off.

Garam just shook his head. Clearly, the Head Augury going missing was not something the local constabulary took seriously. He had to hit them between the eyes with the facts. Claudius decided he had to thump the reality of this matter into their stupid brains and said, loudly and clearly, "He disappeared after performing an augury using a rubber chicken".

Suddenly the entire table where the militia was sitting erupted into action. Dice and cards went spilling onto the ground, along with their wine.

"What!" shouted the Sergent. "Why the Hades didn't you say so earlier. A goddam fake ritual! Unheard of. What sort of bad luck will this bring?"

"The disappearance of the head soothsayer, for one." answered Garam."He was heard screaming as he left that it was the end of Rome, I might add." Garam was smiling the satisfied smirk of a cat that got the attention it wanted.

"Well slave, hurry up and get the details down. We will be onto this immediately!" the Sergent was back at the desk, thumping it for no apparent reason, other than it was HIS desk and he could thump it any time he damn well wanted to.

Chincino looked up, "Can you read?" he asked, innocently. The policeman jumped up to swing a fist at him for speaking. However, Chincino was ready for it and ducked, with a slight sense of satisfaction in his smile as he did so.

"Damn uppity slave! Of course I can't read! No ex-soldier can read or write!" He was shouting so excitedly that his false teeth fell out on the counter. This started his comrades laughing, so he turned around to whip them into shape.

But Garam called the meeting to order. "Look people, it is not difficult. Focus Maximus, the Augury-in-Chief has left his post, a criminal offence as you know. What is more, he left it with his last known words being that Rome was doomed. Now, ordinarily, no big thing, but when the head witchdoctor says it, then runs away, people listen. Gossip gets circulating and the next thing we have panic.

"That means that you Militia will have your hands full. Fires will soon be getting lit, to speed up the end of times, and then looting starts. You will all be working overtime for months UNLESS we can catch this guy before he is out of Rome. Are we getting the picture?" Garam finally got the message across.

The thick brain of the Sergent started to grasp what was happening. The second-in-charge was somewhat smarter than his boss. "But you are the reporter for this, aren't you? I mean, why not simply avoid reporting it? Wouldn't this save everyone trouble?"

Garam was shocked, "You want to silence the press? What sort of low-brow Parthian are you?" he was stunned and deeply horrified at the suggestion. After all, this story was looking to sell a million papyrus by the days end. In the meantime, Chincino was using the wax table to draw a sketch of the fellow, under which he wrote 'This is Focus Maximus' with an arrow rising up pointing at the drawing. He realised there was no point dealing with the men, so he went to the back room and handed it to the secretary, asking her to lithograph it up as a wanted poster.

Then he asked her to fill in a report saying the chief augury had disappeared and to put out an all-points bulletin. The girl was onto it, writing it all up on scraps of papyrus, then tying these to the homing pigeons and setting them off. Out the front the clamour had settled down, so Chincino slipped back in, tugged his bosses sleeve, indicating for them to get out of there.

Garam duly followed, "Well that got them going!" he said proudly, happy with his achievement at getting the Militia motivated.

"That it did, Master. However, WHERE might they be going? The most likely activity will be to go to the local, down some ales, and talk about how they were going to catch the guy, don't you think?"

"Mmm, yes. You could be right there, Chincino. Well, where do you think the Augury will have gone?"

"Perhaps the note he left at the scene might help?" Chincino handed over the scrap of papyrus he tried to give Garam earlier.

"Dammit man!" (Garam takes a swipe at Chincino's head, but misses) He wondered for a moment about how his slave could be so damn quick, then he settled to read the note. His astute eyes, so used to reading between the lines, were trained to grasp what the writer MEANT, not just what they said.

(Now a brief aside to you, dear reader, in order that you grasp what is happening - Latin is a very subtle language. The WAY something was written was more important that WHAT was written. Julius Caesar, when he uttered the famous "Veni Vidi Vici" was not 'really' telling the Senate that he had beaten up some Parthians. He said "I came, I saw, I conquered!" By using the singular possessive form instead of more plural "Vidimus nos vicimus" he was 'actually' telling the "Mos Maiorum" that he was in charge of his army, not them, and that as a result, they had better watch out.)

And so it was with sheer and unadulterated brilliance that Garam grasped the clever word play and came to a stunning conclusion. "Do you think this might be a suicide note, Chincino?"

The slave rolled his eyes, saying "Just what I was thinking, Master."

Patricians were noted for one, specific characteristic - stupidity. Where-as indentured Greek slaves like Chincino were noted for a very different specific thing, the need to survive the stupidity of their Patrician owners.

"Tarquin Rocks, hey? I guess we had better get there. Chincino, flag a chariot, we have to move fast!" The appearance of a Patrician in a chariot roaring through the streets of New Rome, running over the odd Pleb, was not an entirely uncommon one. While it is not really fair to say the Patricians LIKED killing and maiming the Plebs they crushed under the wheels, neither were they overwrought with guilt when they did.

As a result, as soon as a Pleb heard the hooves of two horses and the rattling of metal shod wheels on cobblestones, they all instinctively leapt to one side. What this meant was that the chariot, though an incredibly expensive mode of transport, was amazingly efficient at getting places quickly.

Within minutes they were at the Tarquin, hopping out of their conveyance to find the head augury, who was still making his way to the cliff. Fortunately, he had been stopped from suicide by the prisoners up there, who had recognised his ring of office and begged for some rituals to be performed.

Which was a problem - As the man had taken a vow of silence, they could not quite understand why he said nothing, and they suspected he thought he was better than they were. Subsequently, he was trapped by a circle of very angry inmates, demanding to know the numbers for next weeks lotto draw.

They had found a chicken, gutted it, and were shouting out numbers for the Augury to hold a thumbs up to, or a thumbs down. Which is what Focus Maximus was doing, as he wept. They were so busy writing his answers they did not see the Patrician coming up behind them.

"I bet they are making the common mistake," he says to Chincino. "Why people keep thinking thumbs up is good, and down is bad, I have no idea. Stupid Plebs." He was only thinking of last night, when the priest who was Emperor's representative gave the thumbs down, meaning spare the guys life, but the idiot Gladiator got it wrong - AGAIN - and killed the fellow.

"Let's grab Focus Maximus here, and see what he has to say for himself." They broke up the crowd, who booed and jeered at their intrusion, to find the poor Etruscan looking scared and beaten (possibly because he was and had been) yet appearing not at all grateful to have been saved.

"What is the nearest safe house to here?" Garam asked Chincino as they plucked him from the angry throng.

"Baraka Alashad is close," he replied. Garam nodded.

Good. Baraka was an African prince and, as such, given special status. If he would accept them inside this meant no one could break down the door and demand the Augury for questioning. And further, because he had not left the boundaries of New Rome, the fellow had not yet committed any crime. Technically, the Tarquin itself 'was' a place of exile, therefore by legal definition, outside New Rome, but that would take years for a court to decide. For now, he had the Augury, which meant he had the story.

"You still have the Big Stick?" Garam asked his slave.

"Oh yes, Master. I most surely do!"

Poor Focus Maximus knew what THAT meant and despite his bruises and being saved from certain death by the Tarquin mob, he began wailing loudly over the top of his weeping.

"I thought he took a vow of silence!" Garam muttered as they threw him into the chariot.

Baraka Alashad

The threshold of the rich African Price's home was laden with gold, ivory and incredibly rich objects of art. It took a general calling out about the end of times and the need for safe haven before they got Alashad's attention. The Patrician with his Greek slave and their pet howling Etruscan were given a few minutes to explain why they were there. Intelligent eyes set against a coal-black face bored into them as the man added up the cost versus the benefit of what was being presented.

Chincino guessed words were not going to be enough, so he showed a gold coin to settle the question of admittance and, with Focus Maximus still howling like a dog, they were invited into the astoundingly sumptuous home.

Baraka Alashad bowed, not particularly low, and invited them into the Ante-room. "May I be so impolite to ask for specific details as to why you have the Head Augury here in my house? And please explain why he is so distraught?" he asked.

Garam knew the man quite well, as he had reported extensively (and favourably) on the military campaigns the fellow had run at the behest of Rome in Northern Africa. Baraka was a huge creature, possessing ebony black skin that was wrapped in brilliantly coloured fabrics and topped with a real lions head for a hat. "Nice hat!" the reporter said admiringly.

"I killed it with my bare hands," Baraka modestly responded. "Again, why are we here? Why have you dragged the most respected Priest outside Jupiter Optimax to my house? And WHY is he howling?"

Chincino simply handed Baraka the note the Augury had written. Suicide itself was not a crime, but predicting the end of Rome was considered a terrorist act, one that usually ended with throwing the culprit from the Tarquin rocks.

Obviously, Garam had absolutely no right to usurp justice and leap ahead of it as he was doing but as luck would have it Baraka had absolutely no literacy skills and didn't want to advertise the fact. So he um'd and ah'd a bit and gazed at the note for a while, pretending to look interested.

Then he called over a slave. Curiously, Baraka had only blonde-haired blue-eyed slaves, either male or female. He called all the males, 'Steve-us', and the girls 'Steve-i' - to make sure there was no confusion. Of course, with the lack of schools on the Serengeti, Baraka could not seriously be expected to read, so he let one of the girl slaves whisper the content of the note into his ear while he nodded sagely.

"Thank you Steve-i," he said. Looking up at his guests, he breathed in deeply, considering all the political ramifications, then asked, "What do you propose?"

"We have a bit of a quandary. This prediction will cause trouble, yet it is a fabulous story and will sell a million papyrus. Yet I cannot clarify the matter because Focus here has taken a vow of silence. I need to coax him a little in order to find out what he meant by the 'End of Rome'." Garam explained.

"I would think the term to be fairly self-explanatory, plus might I suggest that the way he howled when you brought him in was hardly suitable for a vow of silence," Baraka noted.

"Oh, I heartily agree, and I did have my slave bring the Big Stick to persuade the fellow to communicate more succinctly. The REAL problem is this, he made the utterance right after a FAKE sacrifice had been offered, with a person using a RUBBER CHICKEN. (Garam emphasised the 'rubber' bit and arched his eyebrows knowingly) It raises several questions that need answering. Surprisingly, the primary one is not necessarily about the accuracy of the prediction. No, the PRIMARY question is to do with how in the democratically elected Presidents name can a FAKE sacrifice with a RUBBER CHICKEN obtain a valid pronouncement of fate." Garam closed his explanation with a quizzical expression.

The huge black man just nodded, rubbing his chin, thinking. He may not be able to read words, but he could read situations like a book. Or not like a book, as he couldn't actually read, but you know what I mean. "I understand. It goes to the heart of Rome, and everything she stands for. If indeed the Chief Augur CAN subsume divine utterance from a rubber chicken, it becomes a slippery slope to anarchy and civil disorder.

"Next we will have people not authorised by the State claiming they too can read divine utterance from things like playing cards, or dice! It would be a New Age, one of utter contempt for authority and the Order of Things. *Les mots et les chose,* becomes jumbled and confused."

He took a flask of wine proffered by a slave called Steve-us and poured some into three beakers, even offering one to Chincino. "Anarchy will rule, the State will collapse, and thousands of years of structure will invert upon itself. We MUST sort out this prophecy and clarify things before we are all doomed."

Steve-us, the one who was in charge of the wine, had read the note over his master's shoulder and cried out, a minore ad maius!" (from the smaller to the greater) They all looked at him, clearing seeing the panic on his face. This underscored the obvious, to stop a general riot this whole thing had to be contained.

"Maybe I should not have published the quote in today's papyrus," noted Garam, casually.

Baraka just looked at him. "The cat is already out of the bag?" he asked. The augur just whimpered and began to howl once more. "Did you really think this through before turning up here?" he asked with a tone of menace in his voice.

Chincino leapt in to save the situation, "Oh great Baraka Alashad, we came here for your sage advice and your tremendous acumen. The spilled milk can only be drunk by the cat that is out of the bag, after all."

The hastily thrown together proverb sounded far more axiomatic than it really was, which was good because it meant the very large and dangerous African would have to stop and think it through. Alashad settled down as he went through the notion, "Mixed metaphor, quite a good twist. I like that. So I presume you are meaning that the Augur here is the cat, while the information is the spilled milk that has escaped. This means if we get the Augur here to somehow suck it back up, reverse his Augury, then everything will be good?"

Chincino had no idea he had said that, but he enthusiastically agreed as it meant they all kept on living a while longer. "Maybe a little wine for our long-suffering Etruscan here?" he suggested.

To whit, the nervous, shaking old man was subsequently plied with a good vintage and told to relax, which he didn't, then told to drink up, which he did. Soon enough he was slurring his wails and becoming far more amenable to reason.

Baraka loomed over the terrified fellow, his great white teeth smiling in what he thought was friendliness, but which only brought to mind the stories of cannibals to the Etruscan. "Now, now my good soothsayer, you have a most excellent reputation. We don't want things getting all sullied and messy because of one small mistake, do we?"

The almost paralysed with fear augury subsequently listened to all sorts of reasons as to why his prediction could not be correct. Either he had performed the ritual using a rubber chicken, which was not permitted, so therefore false and his tongue was already forfeit. Or he lied and created a false prophecy, which meant his tongue was forfeit. The only question was whether he would lose it over the false sacrifice, or the false prediction.

Now, you might have thought that, as he had just been about to end his life, that losing a tongue was a small matter. Especially so since, as he had taken a vow of silence, such a thing would be a positive boon. But Focus

Maximus didn't appear to look at all happy about any positive spin he was being spun.

The fellow gibbered on, mumbling to himself, and vacillating for a few minutes before calling over to Chincino. He made a few gestures in his sign language that the slave translated to the others.

"He is asking for Jupiter Optimax. Something about reversing his vow. It's a good sign!"

"That's about the worst pun I have ever heard," responded Garam.

Alashad just nodded and indicated from one of his slaves to take a chariot to urgently bring the first priest of Rome to their door. They all settled down to a wine or three, casting a collective dour and doubtful look at the still wailing Etruscan.

ooooOOOOOoooo

Soon after there was a clatter of chariot wheels in the courtyard and the Junior consul of New Rome was knocking at the door. The highest priest in the land wasn't actually a priest. Jupiter Optimax was really the Patrician Flavius Corpus, son of Habeus Corpus and, as mentioned, the Junior Consul of New Rome. He had been hastily collected and brought to Baraka's house.

There he found the whimpering Augur, looking disheveled and extremely drunk, wailing on the floor. "Am I correct in understanding he performed an augury over a rubber chicken?" he asked in astonishment. "How on Jupiter's name can we extract him from this? Even if he pronounces the prophecy wrong, we will still have rioting in the streets. How do we get the cat, as you so adroitly put it Baraka old friend, to lick up the spilled milk?"

Baraka gave absolutely no hint that he had just had plagiarised the proverb. But neither did he have any sort of a hint on how to resolve the situation, only that somehow they had to have the Etruscan recant.

Chincino carefully raised a hand, saying, "A suggestion my most high Consul?"

Flavius looked down his nose at the slave who dared speak. Unconscionable behaviour, the man should be flogged, but these were precarious times and the rigid Mos Maiorum needed to be slightly adjusted. He nodded for the slave to speak.

"Well your greatness, perhaps what 'really' happened was that our poor Augur here was a victim of a terrorist plot. It was only an ACTOR who was there, because, after all, no proper Etruscan would ever, in their right mind, give an utterance over a rubber chicken. Perhaps the entire thing was not even a terrorist plot? Perhaps it was just the actors brought over from the old country were performing a joke? They had one of their actors PRETEND to utter a prophecy over a PRETEND ritual, artistic licence and all that. All just a show, part of the act. Do you think this might work as an explanation?"

Chincino improvised on what seemed to him to be the only likely option to get everyone out of the quandary. "All we need here is for Focus Maximus to recant the so-called prophecy and declare it was the result of a hoax, a public relations stunt. Then he lies to say he had nothing at all to do with it." the slave concluded, nudging the Etruscan and indicating for him to agree.

"Sounds reasonable to me," Flavius was known for his practicality. "But first things first, we have to remove the vow of silence the Etruscan took. Therefore, in my role as Jupiter Optimax, I hereby remove the vow. Etruscan, you can speak."

Sadly, and very stupidly, the first thing the Etruscan said was the truth, "But I DID see the signs! Despite it being a rubber chicken, I did see the collapse of Rome!"

Uproar ensued! Slaves began to wail, Baraka lifted his fist, Chincino snatched the old man out of the way, and Garam just sat there not grasping anything. After a few minutes, some semblance of peace returned to the room and the whimpering of the soothsayer settled down to a mere sob.

"This sort of wild prophecy will make the whole economy crash!" cried Flavius Corpus in a despairing voice.

Baraka raised an eyebrow. This might well be the truth! He considered what Jupiter Optimax had just uttered. Was it a prophecy? He then looked at the extremely poor Patrician who had turned up on his doorstep and he started adding two and two. Of course, he did not know what they added up to, but he knew it was something pretty damn good. It got him thinking about how to make a profit from these portents of doom.

At that at that precise moment he started to make a very clever plan.

"He will through life be master of himself and a happy man who from day to day can have said, 'I have lived: tomorrow the Father may fill the sky with black clouds or with cloudless sunshine."

Horace

The Daily Muse

This was a visit Claudius was quite certain he did not want to make. Lord Rupus Murdochius would not normally see a low-grade Patrician like himself, thus he had the vague notion he was in trouble.

The offices of the Daily Muse, publishers of the New Rome Times, were to be found on the venerable Isle of Manhattanus, on the 20th floor of an Insula near to Wall Street and the Financial District. Claudius had been called in to explain his extraordinary actions in permitting one of his clients to perform a fake ritual and he had absolutely no idea what kind of shyte-show was about to go down. Even so, he meekly complied.

As soon as he arrived he knew it had been a mistake. Everyone there was dressing in Togas. Not a modern suit in sight. He had thought the Muse to be progressive, but clearly, it was anything but. Suddenly he felt his white three-piece with a bright yellow tie was not going to be the fashionable statement he thought it would be.

As he walked in through the doors, he saw the large logo of the Muse, embossed in gold and twenty cubitum tall: a huge, drooling fox, with the motto underneath saying " Nam verum esuriit" - 'Hungry for Truth'.

Claudius immediately thought of all the good reputations that this particular Fox had eaten over the years and started to fear his would be the next one served up to the public. But there was no turning back now, he had to try and salvage what he could from the situation. He showed his letter of introduction.

The secretary, blinking twice at his outlandish outfit, spoke into her voice tube, "The Patrician Claudius Hemus Spectre is here to see Lord Rupus Murdocius."

And up he went. A few slaves materialised from nowhere, picked him up, and ran him up to the twentieth floor. He then met another secretary who indicated for him to sit, which he did on a rather luxurious leather lounge. "Lovely chair," he said by way of conversation.

The secretary looked at him as if he were dirt and just said, "Elephant hide. You might take a lesson from its thickness as to what you will need when he sees you."

Suitably terrified, Claudius sat and waited. The ultra-fashionable Cartier water clock dripped, dripped, dripped away the minutes until more than an hour had passed. Claudius was fascinated watching it, mesmerising in its simplicity. He found himself wondering, "They are so traditional, yet they embrace the very latest fashions in clocks?"

Finally, his name is called and he goes to meet his fate. Inside the gold embossed ivory door there is another secretary, who checks his credentials and ID. Then he is frisked for weapons. Lord Rufus was ultra-cautious when dealing with people he did not know.

At last, he is ushered into a vast room. The floor had a superb mosaic depicting the burning of Carthage, and upon it was furniture made of the finest citrus woods. Behind an Arabian rug loomed an enormous ebony desk, inlaid with pure gold showing the sigils of the Fox, and behind THAT sat Lord Rufus Murdocius himself.

He spoke with a broad, aggressive foreign twang, saying in a not very subtle manner, "Why the FOOK did you do it? Are you a terrorist? What fooking reason could ANYONE in their RIGHT FOOKING MIND HAVE AUTHORISED THE USE OF A NON-STATE SANCTIONED SACRIFICE!"

Claudius had expected this was going to be the type of question he would face but, as he went for the long list of excuses he had prepared, words failed him. His boss at GlamorPuss Entertainment told him this was all HIS fault and that he had to go and explain his actions to the real boss of New Rome, Lord Rupus, the man who ran the Muse. Thus he was fully prepared! Sadly, his ability to speak, let alone explain, suddenly dried up.

"What is the matter, man! Taken a Vow of Silence or something! SPEAK UP!" Rupus demanded.

"W-w-w-well, to be fair, it was not meant to be taken s-s-s-s-seriously," he stammered, meekly.

"Goddam stupid idiot Patrician!" Rupus sneered. "Give me a reason why we shouldn't throw you from the Tarquin Rocks?"

"It's not my fault," he whimpered.

Then suddenly Claudius remembered his rehearsed lines."They made me do it. I am very sorry, I will never do it again. Please forgive me. I have learned my lesson and I will never do it again."

The three rules of Roman Law were very clear. When accused, pretend you never heard anything about it. Avoid dealing with the situation. If it can't be avoided, then deny! Deny everything, and admit to nothing. But if you are then proven to be in the wrong, then BLAME. Blame anyone and anything. Finally, when nailed to the cross with no way out, GROVEL.

Clearly, Claudius had gone straight to the grovel stage. However, the next logical step of rolling over onto his back and showing his belly was probably not the smartest thing to do, he reasoned. Despite the extraordinary impulse to do so, somehow he stopped himself from anything other than the far more appropriate falling onto all fours and prostrating himself before the great Lord Rupus.

"I beg you Lord Rupus, have mercy on my soul!" Claudius cried.

The editor of the Muse seemed to take this as normal behaviour and indicated for him to stand. Then, as Claudius did so, Lord Rupus looked puzzled and asked, "What is this ridiculous outfit you have on?"

Claudius got back to his feet and, taking the fact he was still breathing to be an extremely positive sign, looked up and said, "It's called a suit. The latest fashion, much easier to wear than a Toga."

'I could blame the suit,' mused Rupus to himself. The headlines ran through his mind, 'Evil suit takes control of man's mind, drives him insane' or maybe, 'Exotic clothing drives Patrician mad!'. No that won't do it. He needed more. He had a pigeon to hand regarding his reporter now at Baraka's place. The whole thing needed to be contained, yet at the same time, this type of story would sell so many copies it was crazy.

"Rubber chicken? For real, they sacrificed a rubber chicken?" he asked Claudius.

Claudius sensed the possibility of immediate death had retreated, so he found a little courage, at least enough to speak. "Yes Lord Rupus, and I want to say, I did argue that it was a bad idea but they pointed out that legally it was not illegal and they had this objection to killing real chickens."

"Then why didn't they kill a damn goat, or even a rabbit? I mean, rabbits make second rate predictions, but at least it would not have snowballed into this shyte-storm" Lord Rupus said.

"Ah, they didn't like the idea of killing anything at all, for whatever the reason. It was when I pointed out that they HAD to perform a sacrifice that they got the notion of a substitute 'pretend' animal." Claudius clarified.

"So it WAS your idea then?" Poor Claudius nearly lost control of his bowels. Instead, thank the Gods, it was just a fart. But then his heart sank when he realised it was a real stinker.

"Oh by the soul of Optimus Rex, can't you keep control of anything man?" Rupus pressed a button and a slave carrying a torch came in to clear the air. "Look, we have a situation, one where I admit I am torn. On one hand, the story of the decade, the century even! On the other, civil disorder and the ruination of the Empire. "

Finding his voice, Claudius suggested, "Ah, perhaps there are other options? I mean, really, it is just a theatre troupe with a rubber chicken. Maybe treat it all as a farce?"

Lord Rupus leapt up, shouting. "Are you JOKING? The Head Augur reading the entrails of rubber chicken? If this is a FARCE it is a BAD JOKE and DANGEROUS. This is something that strikes at the heart of what it means to be ROMAN! You represent Eruptus Non-Funnius, a small troupe of un-funny comedians that come to New Rome, and who immediately upend all convention. Now they threaten to destroy the Empire. You want us to just pretend these TERRORISTS were joking?"

Claudius was suitably admonished, but a little part of him still saw that too much was being made of this. "This may well be true, Lord Rupus, however, and while it is a very small however, however, it is also a very important one. Do you think, just maybe, that the Etruscan might have been drunk and not noticed? Or perhaps, just overtired? Really, he made one tiny mistake and we are blowing it out of all proportion."

"Mistake? What was the mistake? Reading the rubber chicken sacrifice? Are you suggesting that the leading Augur of Rome does not know the difference between a real and a rubber chicken? I find this even worse than the prediction. Where is our entire society heading when leading figures don't know the difference between a rubber chicken and a living one?

"But worse! What does this say about every single one of his utterances over the last few decades? Everything would be called into dispute. The courts would be full of arguments over decisions made because of his augury. Then THIS would spill out into other predictions and reading of omens. Soon nothing would stand for what it was and everything would be in dispute. You sacrifice a rabbit to see if it is a good day to open a vegetarian plaza and no matter if it is good or bad, people start to question the result!" Rupus was up and pacing around his huge office, waving his arms about, talking about the madness they were all about to descend into.

Claudius set aside the notion of killing a rabbit in front of a vegetarian plaza and certainly put aside the notion of substituting a rubber one, and commented. "Really, it is one small opening of one small coliseum with one small unimportant troupe of unfunny comedians. Do we even need to report it?"

"Silence the press! Are you MAD!" Rupus shouted at him. "What protection will society have from Emperors, Presidents and invading armies if we silence the press!"

Claudius was beginning to understand just how insane the leading people in his society really were. Not to say he didn't know, but to ruin society by publishing that an augury predicted the end of Rome via reading a rubber chicken seemed to be somewhat more of an impost on the social order than simply just not talking about it. "Would it help to say 'I' made a prediction this would not go down well when the troupe originally suggested it?"

"Don't be ridiculous man. You are not qualified to make predictions!"

"Well, to be fair Lord Rupus, neither is the Jupiter Optimax. Really, he is just a junior Consul given a job and is fairly clueless to anything but the most basic signs." Claudius argued.

"EXACTLY! This is precisely the point. If the LEAD augury can make such a basic blunder, everyone else down the chain is even LESS believable. The fall out is enormous, as it destroys the belief people have in the practice of the Augury. Soon people will stop sacrificing and then the end of Rome is certain. Because it is known that if we don't appease the Gods, we are DOOMED!"

Claudius did have a sense of the agnostic regarding the Gods. "Lord Rupus, I know this is what is taught in schools, I understand it is what everyone believes, but in all honesty, there is no evidence to say that sacrifices are really all they are cracked up to be."

"Can you provide any evidence they AREN'T? Do you have some special dispensation from the Oracle of Delphi saying it's all OK not to sacrifice? No, I don't think so." Rupus snorted back at the heresy.

"Well, it would be difficult getting a hall pass from the Oracle. How long since she's been seen? Five Months?" Claudius echoes the obvious, the real reason everyone was so skittish. If it had just been an augury going off his tree, people could get around it, but with the Oracle gone for the first time in three thousand years it was a sign from the Gods no-one could miss. Everyone was on tenterhooks.

"And anyway, how the Hades can you be so agnostic?" Lord Rupus demanded of Claudius. "We have a God for everyone. We have a two-faced God, a warrior God, even a God for sex! We have a drinking God, a God of Money and a God who rules Gods. We even have a poop God to supervise the faeces that will go to those in Hades, so the dead have something to eat! That's the best part about being Roman. A God for every occasion!!"

Lord Rufus was genuinely astounded that anyone could possibly be Godless.

"Lord Rupus, I say my prayers every night, but they are agnostic prayers. Yes, I pray at the altar for everything to go right, but the prayer is: 'Dear Gods, if there are any Gods, save my Soul, if I have a Soul.' This is how I cover all bases."

Lord Rupus just grunts. Patricians are all the same, utterly useless for any real purpose. But they are like the Gods, you need them to keep order. The Plebs need someone to tell them what to do, or else they will sit and do nothing. Now, despite the fact that this was pretty much what they already did, they still needed someone to supervise them. "Well, we have to run the story. I will need you to fill in the background details: how the troupe came to be here, what their idea for the rubber chicken was, and why can't we contact them, etc. So I need you to get up to Baraka's house where my guy is covering the escaping Etruscan story."

"The soothsayer was trying to get out of Rome?"

"Worse, he was about to throw himself off the Tarquin Rocks. Now THAT would have made good press, 'DEPRESSED SAVANT DOES THE RIGHT THING!' but my stupid reporter saved him. Anyway, you are to go to see him up at Baraka Alashad's house."

"The guy that has only white-skinned, blond-haired, blue-eyed slaves?"

"That's the one, up the Palantine, above Bronxinium." Rupus gives him a sheet of directions. "What is the go with the all-white slave thing?"

Rupus shrugs. "Says he hates people with tans. You tell me why people have fetishes and we will both know, but only one of us will care."

Then a buzzer rings, and he looks at a message that comes up the pipe. "Oh shyte no, Trumpetus Orange, the Trumpinius Rex wants to see me." Then he looks up at the fellow still standing there, "What are you waiting for? You get there, give Garam Marsala the background, all the details, and we will see about keeping you out of the bear pits next show, OK?"

"Sure thing, but, er ... I am getting paid for this, yes, Lord Rupus?

"Typical Patrician. Never doing anything just for the good of Rome," he mutters as he writes Claudius a chit.

"Carpe diem, quam minimum credula postero. (Pluck the day
[for it is ripe], trusting as little as possible in tomorrow.)"

Horace

The Outskirts

Meridius gazed out, as she was wont to do, over the fields surrounding the small camp where they were staying. A group of Christians had wanted a performance. After they had heard about the rubber chicken being used, they had told Rufus that paying for Eruptus Non-Funnius to perform would be a good opening act for their next mass.

It was a complete lie, what they REALLY thought was that these poor pagans needed converting. Ofal was miserable, Rufus was annoyed, yet despite everything Meridius quite seemed to enjoy herself.

"It's like a holiday," she said, summing up the situation. "Really, there's no one booing, no one jeering, no one doing anything at all, it is so very peaceful."

"Full of poverty rather than peace," Rufus commented, shaking himself loose from the desire to throttle the neck of their rubber chicken. "We are stuck here, not making any coin, not furthering our fame, and we have to listen to these damn Christians every hour reading one of their gospels. I think lions are too good for them, frankly."

"They seem well-intentioned, Rufus. They do feed us, but I admit that being stuck in this donkey cart does get tiresome. How many days now? Three or Four?" Ofal had forgotten to pack his sundial and had lost track of time.

"Well-intentioned my arse. I can only get a wine if I tell them I believe it is the blood of Jesus," Rufus complained. "I mean, seriously, have these people no concept of PR? How in the name of Jupiter are you ever going to sell wine pretending it is blood! They are entirely bonkers, I tell you."

"Mmmm," Meridius was thinking again, a very dangerous thing. "But they like the rubber chicken thing instead of a sacrifice. That is sweet of them."

"Meridius my dear, 90% of their members are farmers who use being a Christian as an excuse to not to hand over their chickens. I mean, really all this Christ business? So typical with his twelve apostles and rising again from the dead! He even died a martyrs death? It is straight-up Mithraism without the no-sacrifice clause. There is nothing here that Apollonius didn't do better two thousand years ago. It's all cliché' and Pro-forma, PLUS it is ritual cannibalism to boot. But this is not the point. The real thing is how do we get out of here?"

"Oh, good idea," said Meridius.

"What?" replied Rufus.

"We should get out of this cart." and with this, she goes over to the lock, takes a bobby pin from her hair, and picks it open. They are finally out and able to stretch their legs without a supervised toilet break.

"You could have done that days ago," complained Rufus, ungratefully.

"I was enjoying the view," she answered. Just then the alarm is sounded,

"Converts out of the cart!" someone shouted.

The chief priest comes rushing up, using a large stick to politely ask them to hop back in, which did not go down well with Rufus.

Ofal stepped in, to stop the two men from fighting, and offered a suggestion. "Look," he said. "We have been here for a few days, enjoying the food and the company, hearing the wonderful recitals, and I was struck with a powerful message from the Gods..."

"From GOD, the ONE GOD! Haven't you listened to anything?" the priest complained.

"Oh yeah, him or her or it, whatever it might be. Anyway, this God seemed to say something that was entirely reasonable." Ofal said.

"God spoke to you! A miracle!" cried the priest.

Ofal kept the ball rolling, "Oh yeah, fully-fledged miracle, no question. Anyway, he said the truth shall set us free, yes?"

The priest was overjoyed, "Yes," he said, "This is what God said! Everyone, the pagans have been hearing the voice of God! Hallelujah!"

Now a whole gaggle of Christians came sauntering over, shouting "Praise the Lord!"

Rufus was staring suspiciously at Ofal, but he kept on talking, "Yes, he said the truth will set us free, and the truth is, we are cramped up and tired of being here. (the faces in front of him appeared to start frowning) Not that we had anything against the food or the hospitality!" Ofal rushed to add, "But it seems to me that MY God, the one inside telling me what to do, has told me and my friends that we are to walk out of here with all our stuff (he paused) and go back to educating the pagans about this sacrifice business."

Silence greeted this suggestion. Rufus got the idea, and continued. "Of course, we listen to what God tells us, and feel we must obey, but I want you all to know! If, when we walk out of here, if God tells us to turn around, get back in the cart, and listen to stories about Jesus - then this is exactly what we will do. We will come back, get into the cart, and listen. Yes?"

The priest was unsure. He thought about everything the pagans had just said. God DID speak to them and they DID say that if he told them to come back, they would. It all seemed to add up. "But, do you accept the Lord Jesus as your saviour?" he asked.

Ofal saw the escape opening up before them, "I mean, really? God spoke to us and you are asking us THAT question? I am shocked, deeply shocked."

"Of course, of course, I mean, stupid of me really. But do you?" the priest really wanted to make sure their souls were safe, even if it cost them their lives.

Then Meridius chimes in, "Oh he had a chat to me earlier. He was talking about the chaff in the field and sorting things out and where we might find a Samaritan to get a free meal from. Lovely man, very polite."

"Praise be to JESUS!" the priest shouts. He has saved three more lost souls and this is absolutely certain to save him from hell. Without further ado, he hands them back all their gear, and even gives them the donkey cart to carry it with.

"Ah ... I don't suppose a donkey comes with the cart?" Rufus enquires.

It seems that the saving of their souls now qualified them for a donkey, which it did. Thus equipped the trio were back on the road, with the Christians waving gleefully at them as they made their way towards what they guessed was the direction of New Rome.

When they were safely away, Rufus breathed a sigh of relief. "Great work people. I wasn't sure we were ever getting out of there without signing up. They were talking about marrying us all off to members of the tribe you know, and then you really ARE chained up. Brilliant work Ofal, and Meridius, talking to Jesus! What a stroke of genius, they went for it hook line and sinker."

Meridius looked at Rufus oddly, "Well, I only said what he told me to." she explained.

Rufus looked at Ofal, Ofal looked at Rufus, and thought better of saying anything else. Dear Meridius is great for pulling in the crowds, but not all that right in the mental department.

Ofal breaks the ice with a joke, "I heard a good one in the camp - What's the difference between a Goddess and an Angel?" he asked.

"I know, I know!" pipes up Meridius. "A Goddess has bigger tits!"

Rufus roars with laughter, but Ofal looks a little glum, "I thought it was because an angel had wings," he muttered. Then he added, "How the Hades do we know where we are going, anyway? I have no idea where we are, or where the next town might be."

"We just follow the road. I presume, as this is the new country, all roads will eventually lead to New Rome." Rufus replied.

The donkey also seemed quite happy to get away from the Christians and was positively cheerful as it trotted along. Meridius was up front chatting to it like it was a person, apparently disinterested in the fact it never responded. "Look, there's a lovely stone," she would say. Or, "Over there, look at that beautiful tree." Of course, nothing really exciting like Caesar on a bicycle turned up out in the sticks, but the occasional marker stone showed them they were on the right road.

"NR XXI ... 21 leagues to New Rome I reckon that must mean," said Ofal, cheering up as the day progressed. And indeed, after 21 Leagues they came the Nouveau Racine.

"Dammit!" said Rufus, "We are in Canadia, where all the Canadians live.

"I thought it was Canada," said Ofal.

"Stupid. If it was Canada, you would call them Canadans, yes? It is obvious. Canadians live in Canadia, but here we are in Gaulic-Canadia and none of us speak the language. How we are we going set up a show and get in some cash so that we can get back to civilization?"

And just as he said this, Meridius goes up to a lumberjack that was sauntering down the road, and speaks in perfect Gaulish, "Bonjour mes ami. Y a-t-il une auberge près d'ici?" and to both of the lads vast surprise, the fellow seemed to understand it, and directed them up the road.

"What in the name of Zeus was that?" asked Rufus. To say he was surprised was an understatement.

"What was what?" Meridius asked. "Anyhoo, there is an inn we can stay at just up the way. Oh (she giggles) and the fellow did offer me a free place to stay, but I said I had to stay with my friends."

"You were speaking in a strange language, one that fellow understood is what," said Rufus. "I gathered it was New Gaulic by the sleazy way that fellow looked at you."

Meridius treated his comments much like a duck treats water. When they got to the said inn, she kept right on chatting in the strange language and organised for them to stay. She also asked about performances, and if unfunny comedians were needed. She and the innkeeper prattled on for some time, discussing the weather, talking about how busy the roads were, when eventually it came around to the fellow asking who exactly they might be.

"Eruptus Non-Funnius!" the innkeeper exclaims, exploding with excitement. Suddenly he is all over them, hugging, weeping, saying how wonderful it is they came to his humble establishment and did they want anything, food, drink, a better donkey?

Well, it appeared that finally they had landed on their feet. As Meridius explained to them, apparently the troupe had become quite famous in New Rome and were now being hunted by the army as traitors and terrorists.

"Ah, this does not exactly seem a thing we should be ecstatic about," Rufus said quietly. "And why the Hades is he so happy about it and offering us everything like this?"

"Oh," explained Meridius, "In Canadia they hate everything Roman. They are GAULS, you see, and anything that gets up Caesar's nose is a good thing. Because we upset everyone down South, we have been praised and lauded up here. Very logical when you think of it."

The last thing Rufus ever thought of in regards Meridius was logic. "Well, does it mean we get a gig and can earn a few denarii? We can go straight back to the old country from here and avoid New Rome completely."

Meridius laughed, "The innkeeper has sent out a pigeon. In the meantime, he has invited us to stay free of charge, with everything provided, apart from truffles."

"Why not truffles?" asked Ofal, who was clueless in the ways of anything more sophisticated than a pie with a pint.

The innkeeper spoke in perfect Latin, "Because I am not Lord Rupus, you greedy pig!"

Rufus took the queue and explained, "He's an idiot, innkeeper. But you speak Latin?"

"Mais Oui! Do you think I am an ignorant fool!" he snaps back.

"No no no," says Rufus in a conciliatory tone. "I just thought that here you spoke New Gaulish."

"Stupid pig, of course we all speak Latin. We just don't like to." the innkeeper explained.

They were all shown to their room, a large one with an excellent view of nothing at all. There were several beds, a privy, a kitchenette, everything you needed to be comfortable.

"A lot nicer than the cart," said Ofal.

Rufus called a general meeting. He went over the cold facts, the rubber chicken thing appeared to have backfired in a fairly extreme way and going back to New Rome was no longer an option. They would work here, raise some cash, and head straight back to the old country.

Ofal said nothing, Meridius was extremely interested in the paintings on the wall. "I like pictures of snow," she said. "They are always, always so WHITE, yes white. I like that."

Then she looked at the signature and every one of them had a stamp, saying 'Created by the Baraka Alashad Consortium'. As she saw this, Meridius tilted her head and seemed to go off into space.

Rufus was annoyed his plans were not being listened to and he demanded, "Did you even hear a word I said?"

In a deep, strange voice, Meridius replied, "Down the path of eternal Sorrow, through the fires of Hades, Baraka Alashad awaits us."

Not this nonsense again. "Meridius, snap out of it. Everyone knows Baraka Alashad likes white slaves and I promise you, we will avoid his house, OK? What we have to focus on is dealing with the present, the here and now, yes?"

The strange girl then appeared to come back to herself. "I love snow, do you think it will snow?" she asked.

"Good God, this is Canadia woman, of course it will snow." he snorts back.

Rufus did find himself somewhat discombobulated by his associate's strangeness on occasions, but at the same time, she was wonderful in front of a crowd. Soon the good news arrived, they had been booked for the local 'Quebecois' coliseum for a solid three months.

The bad news, they really, really wanted Focus Maximus to do the augury every evening. The one thing the Canadians wanted to hear more than anything was that Rome was going to fall, but they wanted it from an authoritative source.

Rufus was scratching his head at how on earth this was going to happen when there was a knock on the door. He opened it to find an enormous man standing there, legs apart, arms on hips and kitted out in what was obviously a rather tattered Roman army uniform.

"Brutus Maximus, at your service!" he bellowed in a voice designed to be heard across mountain ranges.

"A shoe that is too large is apt to trip one, and when too small, to pinch the feet. So it is with those whose fortune does not suit them."

Horace

Brutus Maximus

Some might say he was a small mountain, others would agree and add that he was almost as smart. Brutus Maximus was a big boy with a big voice, one that seemed to echo off the walls as he spoke. He was not clever, witty, charming or urbane but he did possess one remarkable attribute: an enormous capacity for, and a love of, killing things.

People talk about the enlightened age where intelligence ranks above the brute, well this was not our friend Brutus, not at all. He possessed a huge round face that seemed to have a perpetual smile on it, one littered with a variety of teeth, or so it seemed. "This one," he would say, pointing to what was clearly the tooth of a bear, "I had implanted by an Etruscan after I had an argument with a bear. He knocked one of my teeth out, so I knocked one of his, and we called it square. As a token of respect, I had this one fitted."

And so on he would go, describing how every tooth had arrived. But apparently he was not here to talk about teeth. He was there to talk generally about whatever passed through his rather diminutive mind.

Rufus was somewhat trying to avoid letting him into their room, but it made little difference, the fellow just walked in, bellowing how wonderful it was to meet the famous troupe.

"Did you know that in the distant past," he said, "HUGE creatures roamed the earth. They were called dinosaurs, and they were so large they eventually self-immolated, leaving only their bones behind."

It appeared to be an exceedingly important fact, but Rufus could not see why. "Ah, a creature so large that it ignited itself and burnt up seems a little, shall we say, odd."

"I thought exactly the same thing, but a professor said it. So it must be true." he bellowed right back.

"What university does he attend?" Rufus asked, politely.

"Ho ho ho," laughed Brutus. "He'd already finished university, didn't I mention he was a professor?"

"Yes, I was wondering where he was certified, that was all," said Rufus sarcastically.

Sarcasm, or any form of wit that did not involve bludgeoning topics with opinions simply passed by Brutus like a fart in the wind. If he got any scent about what you meant, it was gone before the brain realised it was there. "But enough small talk, let's get down to why I am here," his bellow did not seem to lessen despite the immediate proximity of three other sets of ears.

Rufus waited, Brutus said nothing. He waited a little longer, indicating with his hand for Brutus to continue. Finally the fellow got the message,

"Oh, yes, the reason I am here. I forgot for a moment and was enjoying the wonderful snow on those pictures."

"Aren't they lovely," piped up Meridius. "You would see quite a bit of snow up here, I would imagine"

Oddly enough, when faced with a pretty girl Brutus suddenly seemed at a loss for words, "Um, ah, um, ah yes, yes I do." he stammered.

"A big strong man like you must wrestle many bears, I would also imagine." she continued.

"Ah, um... yes... many bears." he started to get embarrassed and blush.

"Oh by the GODS!" exclaimed Rufus. "WHY are you here?"

"Oh yes, revenge. I had heard about Eruptus Non-Funnius, the unfunny comedians, and it was in fact my uncle, Focus Maximus, who gave the prediction that created all this trouble. Now, just because he has ignored me my entire life, this did not mean he should not be saved. I had a dream that I was to rescue him, and by the Gods I am going to! Obviously, you lot showing up in my home town was a clear message you had come here for my help." Now Brutus was back on track, his shyness evaporated and his gusto returned.

"And what, dare I ask, has this to do with us?" asked Rufus.

"Well he is YOUR friend, I presumed you would want to help him," responded Brutus.

"He doesn't know who we are, nor would he care, and it was his pronouncement about the end of the Empire that has us being called terrorists and therefore hunted by New Rome. It is not really the stuff friendship is made of, nor does it precipitate a desire to get oneself killed saving someone you don't know." Rufus laid it all out so Brutus could see the full picture.

"Exactly," he roared back, absolving himself of all reason. "He made you famous, so you owe him. And because I am his relative, you owe ME to help get him out."

This was not exactly the sort of logic the Rufus considered sound, yet when a very large man who appears to enjoy killing things says you owe him a defacto favour, it is very difficult to put your objection to this into words that won't get you dead. "Ah, and where exactly might your uncle be?"

"He is at Baraka Alashad's house, in New Rome," Brutus said.

Ofal had just been sitting in the background avoiding everything, but he suddenly chirps up, remembering the fateful pronouncement made by Meridius just moments before. "Down the path of eternal sorrow through the fires of Hades, Baraka Alashad awaits us."

"Fantastic!" exclaims Brutus, apparently not hearing any trace of negativity what-so-ever in these words. "Let's get packed. I have a boat all ready to go!"

Rufus just shook his head. They were trapped. If the gig promised here in Canadia was to come about, they needed Focus Maximus. If they wanted to get back home, they needed the money from this gig. It seemed the Gods had conspired to force them back to New Rome after all.

"A cultivated wit, one that badgers less, can persuade all the more. Artful ridicule can address contentious issues more competently and vigorously than can severity alone."

Horace

Back in New Rome

G aram Marsala did not like having another Patrician around, not one little bit. They are like cats, perfectly good when around lesser animals, such as dogs and humans, but another Patrician? No, never a good thing. There is good reason why assassination was the preferred form of suicide in New Rome, which all boils down to the fact there are too many Patricians.

Chincino, in the meantime, was acting as the intermediary.

"So," Garam said with an undisguised sneer to his slave, "In reference to the so-called fashionable clothes he is wearing, please suggest to my DEAR friend here, but in your most sarcastic tone, the words: 'SO! You are non-traditional? I guess that is why you recommended the rubber chicken?'."

Chincino obliges, using his best sarcasm to make oblique stabs at the reputation of the other Patrician. Claudius knew this game, "So, perhaps you could say to my beloved New Roman patriot the following: 'As a working Patrician, what is it that leads you to this vast jumping to conclusions? Is it because you are a mere JOURNALIST?'. " he sneered right back at Chincino, who did his best to pass along the sneer as well as the words.

"Please ask my trusted and respected comrade here the following, if you could my dear Chincino: 'Odd, I don't believe 'I' am the one implicated in a TERRORIST PLOT!'." Garam re-sneered.

Finally, Chincino gave up and said, "Why don't you just talk to each other. I mean, you are both here in the same room."

And so they stopped talking to stare venomously at each other, which was when Baraka entered the room to break the tension.

Their perfect host simply suggested they come in for some wine. Claudius then explained to Baraka that he had been sent by Lord Rupus with information about the plot to destroy New Rome, which was to be given to the 'other' Patrician in their presence.

Baraka sat them both down and smoothly poured oil over the troubled waters. Though in this case, it was more wine than oil he poured. "Gentlemen, I am given to understand that you BOTH want a solution to this rather vexing problem. Of course we all do, so may I suggest that we turn the lemons we have been handed into lemonade."

Chincino translated his words for them, "Baraka Alashad here is offering you both an opportunity to make money."

The suggestion of making a profit is like an automatic switch to a Patrician. Suddenly they forgot their differences and were all ears.

"I can see you might be interested in lending me an ear," Baraka says casually. So he seats them, gets a decent wine from the cellar, but more importantly, he has it poured by a completely naked blonde-haired, blue-eyed and extremely pretty girl slave.

(He guessed this lot preferred girls. Of course, the REAL reason for the white slaves was exactly this, to distract his guests while he extracted information or money.)

At the same time, he ushers Chincino, the only one present with any intelligence, out of the room. "My dear slave, you need to rest, so go have a bath and prepare to serve us dinner, if you would be so kind."

Chincino looks over to his master, Garam, who waves him off. The Patrician is far more eager to hear how they will make money. The two sleazy Patricians were now on their own, getting drunk and so busy ogling the naked blonde that they just nodded a 'yes' to everything Baraka was saying, without actually listening.

"So, as Patricians, poor Patricians, what you really need is real estate, yes?" (they nod yes) "And as an African, I don't have an actual right to buy property in the central district, do I?" (they nod yes) "And with all this kerfuffle about the end of times, the Empire failing, people will be keen to get out of real estate and into gold, won't they?" (they nod yes while looking at the magnificent breasts of the girl who seems to be showing such interest in them) "So what we need to do is use YOUR good names to scoop up the bargains, yes?" (they nod yes while she brings in another one, and they both sit bare-assed naked on the patricians laps, giggling)

"Excellent, so if you would like to play with these girls here, all you need do is sign this small agreement..." (they take up the pen and sign while the girls lick their ears.).

"Marvellous work gentlemen, absolutely a pleasure doing business with you." He claps for the gorgeous girls to leave and, half-plastered, the two Patricians (who have by now decided that they are both excellent fellows) remember they just signed something to do with those girls who were now leaving.

"Er, what did we just sign?" Garam asks.

"Your lives away," said Baraka smiling.

They both do a classic double-take, "What?" they both ask in unison.

"It's not so bad as all that. What we agreed to do, as we discussed, was to purchase property in both your names as and when the market crashes, as it will. Obviously, you both are too poor for any such thing, so I am providing you all the funds. I will be bartering my extensive pile of gold when the price soars, as it always does in extreme situations, in exchange for real estate. The deeds I will be putting in both your good, Patrician names. Now, in return for the amazingly comfortable existence you will be getting, you have become my indentured slaves. It's a sort of loan agreement where YOU are the collateral." Baraka explained. "Oh, and as a matter of course, your slaves are now transferred over to myself. Chincino, come in."

The freshly pampered and washed slave, who just happened to be white, blonde-haired and blue-eyed did come in and had it explained how his ownership had just now been transferred.

"I was just thinking that this was a great idea coming here," he said to Baraka Alashad.

"What did you do before you became indentured?" the black man asks.

"Oh, I was a solicitor," Chincino says.

"I need to speak to my solicitor!" exclaimed Claudius, remembering it was Chincino.

"How convenient, we have one here. Chincino, if you could just witness this document. (he does) And now you will note Clause 196-B and can you please subsequently advise our dear Patricians that they also signed a waiver for legal advice." replied Baraka.

"Well, former Master, this is exactly what you have done," Chincino explains.

"You bastard!" declared Garam.

"Now now, no need for slander," Chincino advises. Baraka just smiles his warmest smile,

"Thank you, Chincino. Please get these papers filed. And my dear Patricians, it has been a pleasure working with your good selves as well."

In a back room, Focus Maximus cried out, "We are all DOOMED! The Empire is DOOMED!" All four men look at each other as Claudius finds his voice.

"What the HADES is this all about?" Baraka explains.

"In a nutshell? Sitting here I came to understand that Focus Maximus has inadvertently done us all a tremendous favour. I now WANT the whole thing to come crashing down in a panic. Why? Because people will sell off Real Estate for nothing when the sky is about to fall on them. That way I get to suck up all the best real estate, because NOW I can buy the good stuff normally proscribed to non-Patricians."

"Allow me to explain." Baraka is as smooth and unruffled as an egg that has not fallen off a wall. "What we have here with our slightly mad Head Augury is a MASSIVE opportunity (they all reach and touch the Lord Ops around their necks, saying 'Bless the Lord Ops') to make vast amounts of money. I have gold, you two have names no-one suspects. The deal, as you have signed it, is very fair.

"Soon enough the system will right itself. After the price of real estate triples, as it will, I will sell off most of your holdings. With this money you will be able to free yourselves from indenture, plus you end up with a property each, gratis. In short, because you have lent me your names to invest in city real estate, I end up with pots of Denarii to bath in and you get a house. It's good for everyone."

Then he pauses, and turns to his new solicitor, "Perhaps you could advise them on their rights at this point my dear Chincino?"

"Just what I was thinking myself, Master." Chincino echoes. "You don't have any," he explained.

"But, no one read me my Carmen Miranda rights!" spluttered Claudius.

"What," asked Chincino, "The right to wear fruit?"

"It is courage, courage, courage, that raises the blood of life to crimson splendor. Live bravely and present a brave front to adversity."

Horace

Trumpetus Orange

Lord Rupus did not like him. No one LIKED him, but you could not refuse an audience when he called you in for one. The arrogant, stuffed up, orange-haired madman was rich beyond Croesus. So rich, that when he farted, you inhaled and said 'thank you'. So rich that if he pissed on you, you called it your daily wash. So rich that when he made love to your wife, while you were watching, you simply asked if he wanted your daughter as well.

Trumpetus Orange was venal, crass and blunt. You knew he was a bad man because he was nasty to puppies that were not pedigree. But he was rich, so damn rich, that what he said mattered. "Look," he said to Lord Rupus, "We work together on this and the money we make will blow your mind. And I mean, BLOW your MIND. How often had the Head Augury predicted the end of the Empire? (Lord Rupus had no idea) Seventeen times in the last two thousand years. And what has happened after this? (Lord Rupus had no idea) The real estate market plummeted, then the stock market crashed, but the price of gold went through the roof."

"And your point?" Lord Rupus asked.

"MONEY! What other point is there? We need to control the information so we can control the panic. We want to create a bubble of fear, but we want it timed so that we are in the best position to capitalise on it. Let me explain how it works."

Trumpetus brings Lord Rupus into an adjoining room, where a model of New Rome was displayed. His bright orange hair and not-so-bright orange skin was either an overdose of carrot juice, or a really bad fake tan. As health did not seem a priority for the man, Lord Rupus guessed fake tan.

"Ok then, let's say TOMORROW (Trumpetus emphasises tomorrow as if it is important) you write up a piece that the Head Augury is captured, but refuses to recant. OK? Now what THAT does, and I know all the statistics, I got all the best statistics, what THAT does is cause a mild ripple. People hear it, but they don't believe it. Now what 'I' do will start the ball rolling. I pretend to go into a panic, and order the wholesale selling of all real estate assets, taking only gold for exchange. You got that?"

Lord Rupus nods his agreement.

"Good, then the NEXT day, the headlines read that Trumpetus Orange must know something because he is selling off all his assets. What THIS does is cause the rich people to list houses, and buy into the Stock Market.

Why do they do this? Because they start taking up GOLD. Everyone in the know, knows what will happen. The lower classes won't get it and will stupidly believe the whole thing will blow over. But with the rich selling all their real estate to buy gold, the housing price falls and the stock market surges. Now I get HUGE bids for gold, and cash up massively.

Then, on the third day, you release this fact to the public." Trumpetus smirks, his utterly confident confidence was both alarming and comforting. "And you know what, when people hear I have gone there, they will all believe that it is real. They will all run for gold flogging off their houses for next to nothing in order to get to the safety of precious metals. That way, all the good real estate comes on the market cheap. But here's the rub, no one is buying. The price drops, and over the next week, as the gold price escalates, people just want OUT of real estate.

"Every day, you keep reporting and reporting how everything is going South. Was it because the Head Augury was right? Maybe the Empire is finally done? Then the coupe de gras, you publish that you are getting out of New Rome and heading for your hidey-hole in the Bahamus. So long, and thanks for all the money.

"That will be IT, the market crashes, real estate is worth nothing, and gold is worth everything. I exchange my gold for property." Trumpetus ends his soliloquy with a small bow. But not too much of one, else he appear humble.

"And why should I go along with you on this?" Lord Rupus asked the obvious question.

"Because at the same time you do exactly as I am doing and you will make pots and pots of Denarii!" Trumpetus laughs. "Are you IN?"

"You think I am willing to exchange my good name, the great and longstanding name of the New Rome Times, and my entire sense of decency just to make money?" he asked.

Trumpetus nodded enthusiastically, "Of course! Why else would we be talking?"

Lord Rupus looked at that orange hair suspiciously. Was it really his? It looked more like he implanted some monkey hair. But pulling himself from the distraction, his mind went over the facts. "And if I don't go along with this, then my offices will suddenly get trashed by ravaging hordes of mindless plebs living in fear of the consequences of the Head Augury."

Trumpetus clapped his hands for wine. "Precisely, so we all understand how easy this is. Lord Rupus. This is the opportunity of a lifetime, no, of several lifetimes if you believe the Buddhists. So I ask again, are you IN?"

"Yeah yeah, I am in. I don't like it, though. You are putting a gun to my head."

"I am putting a fist full of Denarii in your bank," Trumpetus said plainly. "Look, if we don't control this, if we don't manage this collapse, then it will happen anyway and everyone will be the worse for it. This is a controlled let down where the few in the know will do incredibly well. The market will crash anyway, we are just putting ourselves in the driving seat of the donkey cart."

"The cart that is about to fall off a cliff?" Lord Rupus clarified.

"Exactly! I knew you would understand. Here, this is the press release for tomorrow."

Trumpetus drank down his non-alcoholic wine and said he had work to do, which was his way of saying 'thank you for your time, now piss off'. Lord Rupus did not like it, but he had learned, to survive you rolled with the punches. Trumpetus was right and the thing to do was to stay ahead of the curve. He already knew how dangerous this entire business was, but the headline was priceless.

He looked down at what Trumpetus had written: "Rubber Chicken, the Terrorist No-one Ever Suspected" Not bad. But it needed reworking: "Rubber Chicken Terrorist Threatens New Rome!" There, much better.

Taking a chariot back to his offices, Lord Rupus ducked into a pigeon shop and sent a secret memo to all offices. "Sell everything! Buy Gold!

Saepa stilum vertas, iterum quae digna legi sint scripturas.

(Turn the stylus [to erase] often if you would write something worthy of being reread.)

Horace

The Road to Hades

Flavius Corpus, New Rome's Jupiter Optimax, had returned home and was walking about his lobby with extreme agitation. The stupid damn Etruscan refused to recant. Yes, it would mean they would cut out his tongue, but didn't the man grasp just how much fuss and bother was going to happen now?

It was incredibly selfish of the fellow to obstinately stick to his prediction. And as for that nosey reporter! How DARE he interrupt the will of the Gods. If the augury wanted to kill himself, why stop him? A dead Etruscan would simply mean things would settle down, and the whole thing would have blown over as just another nutter with crazy talk. But NOW he was in the hands of the worst possible person in all of New Rome, Baraka Alashad.

This all meant there was nothing else for it, he needed to go down to the Cross Roads Tavern and order up an assassination. He had a private chariot, so getting to the outskirts of the city only took an hour or so.

Once there he followed the usual procedure: look straight ahead while sitting down at the front bar, drinking some mead. Every sip he would take from the horn he was provided ended with him tapping the bar three times. No more than three rounds of three and, if an assassin was present, he would introduce himself.

Well, of course there was an assassin present. The place was packed full of ex-soldiers all looking to make a Denarii or three. Flavius didn't get past the second tap of the first round before he had a throng six deep around him, all holding their hands to their chests going 'Ave Caesar!' He HAD wanted to keep the matter quiet, but that was never going to happen now.

"Who's it to be, Gov? Big and important costs lots. Wife costs loads. Tax officials are free." The bartender homed in on the money. This was obviously the man who coordinated things. "Greekus Todius at your service 'person we never saw' and who we will never recognise in any lineup." He nods his head, taps his nose, and points his finger as if to say it was all a complete secret, and waits.

Flavius is somewhat overwhelmed and is at a loss for words. Greekus helps him out, "First time assassination? Well, never you mind, we are used to that. Just give us the name, what the person's job is, and we will quote you a price."

"Um, Focus Maximus," Flavius says, not knowing any other way to broach the sensitive subject of killing the Etruscan nuisance. But he is greeted with silence.

"What? The guy who said the Empire was gonna fall and all?" a voice from the crowd asks.

"Er, yes." Flavius answered.

"But we LIKE the idea of the Empire falling on its arse. Why you want to go kill him then?" said another voice.

Clearly, Flavius had chosen the wrong den of assassins. But given that he was IN a den of Assassins, he needed to tred carefully. "Well, it's nothing personal," he explained.

"How could it NOT be personal?" yet another voice piped up. "You want him DEAD! That's pretty personal."

Flavius was starting to be concerned for his own safety at this point. Squirming on his seat, holding his partly drunk horn of mead, the Jupiter Optimax was starting to look like a runner. The bartender decided 'he' needed to take charge of proceedings. After all, money is money and, even if you like the target, when you are paid to do a job you do it properly.

"Now now gentlemen. We have a paying customer, no need to badger him about the choice of target. We are all professionals here, I don't need to remind you. Let's get to the important part," and looking at Flavius he asks, "What are you prepared to pay, Roman?"

The whole thing about being Jupiter Optimax was that you were supposed to represent Jupiter, the two-faced God. Now, while he had never met Jupiter, Flavius was more than capable of being two-faced. "Oh don't get me wrong, I love the prediction. The problem is that the bastard wants to RECANT!" said Flavius, lying through his teeth. "Now, like all of you, a bit of fire, the burning of New Rome, that really gets my juices flowing, but if he RECANTS, then nothing happens. It all goes away. We don't want THAT do we lads?"

"Noooo!" they all cheer, happy that everyone is on the same team.

Greekus is unmoved by the words, and once more asks, "How much, Roman?"

"A talent of gold," Flavius says, feeling unbelievably generous with the gold he was about to melt down from Temple of Moneta.
"Five!" Greekus counters the offer with his insanely over-priced demand. "He's famous, we could get into a lot of trouble, so you have to make it worth our while."

The whole bar is suddenly silent, Flavius feels the sweat on his brow. "That is outrageous!" he says, on impulse. Then he realises calling a hundred or so assassins outrageous was not a particularly good idea. "But entirely fair. I will have to melt down a few statues, of course, but hardly anyone goes to worship at Moneta's temple anyway, so we should be good."

Greekus spits on his hand and offers the handshake to seal the deal. Flavius accepts it, cringing at the germs he might be contracting through his skin at that point. But it was done, the Etruscan would be removed, the gossip would cease, and everything would settle back down. Everything he did was for the good of New Rome and the glory of the Empire, and the cost was merely one small life of a stupid Etruscan who foolishly decided to read the entrails of a rubber chicken.

The road to Hades WAS paved with good intentions, after all.

"The descent into Hell is easy"

Virgil

Row Your Boat

Rufus really hated rowing, while Brutus appeared to thoroughly enjoy it. They had caught a courier ship to New Rome, leaving most of the props back on the wagon under the careful gaze of their innkeeper. The fellow seemed so entirely pleased they were going to get the Etruscan that he even gave them a packed lunch. Canadians were such a strange and helpful people. It was something that Rufus would never comprehend, but at the same time, don't look a gift horse in the mouth, unless you are a Trojan.

Brutus was bellowing away, as usual, quoting some of the extraordinary truths that only he seemed to know. "Did you know that New Rome has stockpiles of Gold so huge that you could pave a road from here to the Moon with it?"

How a road to the moon was going to be built was never explained, or even why you would want to waste all that gold paving it. However, facts and reality seemed to be two entirely different animals that lived either side of the world where Brutus existed.

"I am studying to be a blacksmith, you know," he bellowed.

"How uninteresting," said Rufus.

Brutus then went to great lengths to explain the types of metal and at what heat they had to be before you could hit them, which you could tell by the colour of the metal. He appeared to know just about everything you could possibly know about blacksmithing, but when Rufus finally asked, after three hours of monologue, what Brutus had actually made, the man smiled and pulled forth a rather sad looking knife.

"Isn't it a beauty!" he shouted at poor Rufus.

The man was clearly proud of his achievement. "Ah, lovely. So, this is the sort of thing you make?"

"Absolutely, took me four years of study to learn how to do it. Only cost me ten thousand Denarii for the equipment, but now I have the technique, I can make thousands of them!"

"How many have you made?" Rufus really didn't care, but he felt as if he were obliged to ask, and it was mind boggling boring just rowing.

"One!" Exclaimed Brutus, apparently believing this to be a tremendous achievment.

"Pray tell me, what is that one knife worth?" Rufus knew he shouldn't ask, but he wondered when or even if the reality of math would ever occur to the loud giant beside him on the rowing bench.

"I can get TWO Denarii per knife," Brutus says proudly.

"So, after five thousand knives, you will have your money back?" Rufus questioned.

"Oh no, it doesn't work like THAT!" exclaimed Brutus. "You see, when I show some rich person my knife, he always presumes I am going to kill him, and he donates large amounts of money to my cause," Brutus explains.

"Your cause?" Rufus asks, perplexed, but at least he understands how Brutus makes a living.

"Yes, the 'feed Brutus' charity. It is very well supported you know."

"I am quite sure it is," Rufus added dryly.

"LAND HO!" a call comes up from the coxswain. New Rome was in sight, along with the remarkable statue of Caesar in his robe, with his bike, but this time he is holding up a torch.

"Oh look, a really, really big statue of Caesar," said Meridius from up the back of the bank of oars. "I was told that the Gauls donated that to the city. Wasn't that sweet of them?"

Gauls being sweet? Rufus could think of no other person in the entire world who would describe that ornery bunch of argumentative cheese eaters as being sweet. However, the main issue was in front of them. He was just glad to be off the oars and yet also extremely trepidatious about stepping into New Rome - possible because they were all under the sentence of death.

"Indubitably tantamount to an interesting few days," said Ofal, using his word from last week alongside the new word for this week.

"We need to be careful," said Rufus. "Keep a low profile, draw no attention to ourselves. We must quietly get to this Baraka Alashad's house, pluck out the Etruscan, and get back to the boat without anyone realising we are here." All of which were impossible demands with someone like Brutus in tow.

"Look," said Meridius as they pulled up to the wharf. "They have little statues of the 'Caesar of Liberty' for sale. How lovely!"

Brutus, of course, went straight to the nearest bar, telling the party to call him when they found out where the house was. Which was Canadian for 'I am drinking now, so call me tomorrow, sometime, or the day after'.

Rufus suspected his determination to save his uncle was more about a holiday to New Rome than anything to do with helping a relative in distress. Regardless, they made inquiries, found out where the house was, and made their way back to the bar, only to find it completely empty.

"Where did everyone go?" he asked the barman.

The fellow looked up and said, "Apparently they have all gone off to get Focus Maximus, who is hiding at Baraka Alashad's house."

Rufus was amazed that the incredibly stupid Brutus could have organised his way out of a wet paper bag, let alone complete the mission so quickly. But he was suspicious, "What precisely do you mean by 'get Focus Maximus'?" he asked.

"Oh, standard assassination. Some rich Roman, whose name I can't mention, has been stupid enough to offer five talents of gold to have him done in."

The blood drained from his face as Rufus suddenly realised the strange comment from Meridius may well have been prophecy. Without Focus Maximus, they had no show in Quebec. No show in Quebec meant no passage home. No passage home meant someone was going to murder all of them. It was getting complicated.

"I don't suppose the person who can't be mentioned has a name?" he asked, wondering if the barkeep was as stupid as he looked.

"Ho ho, nice try young Sir! But when it is the Junior Consul you make sure your lips are sealed. No names for you!" The barkeep radiated his cleverness at seeing through their ploy.

"Loose lips sink ships, and all that," nodded Rufus.

The barkeep winked back.

Rufus bundled them all outside to organise a plan. Ofal summed up the situation,

"Indubitably Tantamount to a problem, hey?" Rufus looked at him dolefully.

But Rufus had clicked into hero mode. Action was the only thing that mattered now! "Get a chariot, we need to reach Baraka's house first."

Fl ctere si n queo s peros Acheronta movebo
— If I cannot move heaven, I will raise hell.

Virgil

Assassins

The assassins sauntered along quite happily, possibly because they were all extremely drunk, but also because of the excellent fellow they had fallen in with. When he told them he was here to get Focus Maximus, they all cheered. When he said he was going to Baraka Alashad's house, they all cheered. When he said they should ALL go, they all cheered again, and left.

Obviously dear reader, you would understand the miscommunication that was underway and we can easily predict that, at the point of arrival, when the assassins were expecting a good murder dear Brutus would be expecting something entirely different.

As the facts stood, he presently believed he had fallen in with a wonderful group of fellows, all ex-army and all who loved to drink. What more could you want? He had completely forgotten about Eruptus Non-Funnius and any recollection of his erstwhile travelling companions was now but a distant memory.

The ragtag collection of misfits sauntered along at an easy pace, laughing and joking and telling bawdy tales of their various conquests, both in the army and in the bedroom, most of which were lies, and all of which were exaggerations.

When finding out about the incredibly benevolent chap who was offering five talents of gold to extract Focus from the clutches of the evil Baraka, he asked one of his new-found friends, "Who is paying all this money to get Focus Maximus?"

"None other than the Junior Consul. He popped into the Cross Roads Tavern to solve the problem of the Etruscan who was going to recant. We can't have Head Auguries recanting now, can we? You wouldn't know WHAT to believe if they can't get their entrails right."

Something deep down in the rather small brain of Brutus Maximus started to twig that things might not be as they seem. High Born Patricians only every went to the Cross Roads Tavern when they needed someone done away with. It would seem unlikely someone would pay anyone five talents of gold to merely pluck a person from a house.

But then he understood. "There must be a lot of guards up there protecting that house?" he asked.

"Oh yes, loads. Baraka stores his gold there and has a huge number of people running security." his drunken friend slurred.

Well, that would explain why there were so many of them. If it was just an assassination, only one would have gone and snuck in. Obviously, they need to put up a big show of force to make sure they hand him over without too much bloodshed.

Happy that he had understood things correctly, Brutus points out yet another bar they can drink dry before moving on up the Palatine. The sign outside said, "Hard Rock playing tonight!"

Which is exactly what it was, and they all partied out to Hard Rock which was, literally, convicts hitting rocks with hammers, but with great rhythm. A good drinking session with cheering and sculling and generally laying waste to the bar furniture ensued.

No one noticed the Chariot and the look of utter panic on the face of one of its occupants racing past as they partied on, nor did anyone in the chariot pay any attention to them.

On matters of survival, the leader of the Eruptus Non-Funnius troupe could be quite focused. Rufus needed to get there, save the Etruscan who created all this trouble for them, and get away before dawn. It was early evening already, but with luck, they would catch the midnight run to Canadia and be back inside two days.

Ira furor brevis est. animum rege: qui nisi paret Imperat.
(Anger is a brief madness: — govern your mind
[temper], for unless it obeys it commands.)
Horace

Baraka Understands

The cool of the evening began to dip through the olive groves on the edge of town. The chariot clipped to a stop and the driver leaned over with his palm upwards for payment. Rufus went to his purse, to find it rather devoid of Denarii, "Just a minute," he lied. "I will pop in and collect a few coins." And with this he bundled Ofal and Meridius off the back, nodding in a friendly manner towards the extraordinarily doubtful face of the charioteer.

Meridius said, fairly audibly, "Why would Baraka pay our fare?" She was reasonably clueless to the ways of the world and Rufus was frankly surprised she even considered the notion of paying a fare at all, but he shunted them towards the doorway, even so.

He would think of something, but the truth was, he was running on panic. As you may or may not be aware, panic causes a surge of adrenaline. In the case of a mother having to lift a huge boulder to save a child, it can give extraordinary strength. In the case of Rufus trying to find a way not to die, it gave him a vast supply of foolish hope.

He knocks on the door, a white, blonde-haired, blue-eyed slave answers, and Rufus blurts out, "We are here for Focus Maximus!"

Most would agree, it was not exactly a clever approach, but by pure circumstance, as the Slave was shutting the door in his face, Baraka himself happened to be walking by. He found himself curious as to who would be on his door and came out to see for himself.

"Who might you be?" he said with a tone that was both threatening and regal.

Rufus looked over his shoulder and realised there were several slaves there with large clubs. Then Ofal tapped him on the shoulder, indicating for him to look about. Rufus immediately wished he hadn't, as an even larger number of well-muscled white men with clubs started to form up behind them.

On the positive, it would stop the charioteer from killing them, he supposed. In the negative, this would be because they were already dead. However, right now his adrenaline decided that as running with his feet would not work, running with his mouth might. "Eruptus Non-Funnius at your service, Sir!" and he bows low to whom he presumed to be Baraka Alashad. "We are here to warn you that a large troupe of angry assassins are on their way to kill Focus Maximus, who we understand is in your care."

"And?" Baraka asks, still waiting for a good reason for them to be on his doorstep. Rufus did not quite expect a question like 'and?' which was unfortunate, because he had nothing else.

However, Meridius spoke up, once again in that strange guttural voice she used, "The Augury, Baraka Alashad."

You may have thought such a comment would put the fellow off-side, considering he was set to make a fortune by keeping the augury all to himself, but the huge African then did an extraordinary thing.

His eyes popped open like a champagne cork exploding from a bottle and he dropped to one knee in subservience. "Your Grace, I am humbled. Please enter my household and accept my hospitality."

To say Rufus was confused and Ofal downright confounded was an understatement, but they were ushered in, with him briefly saying, "Ah, the charioteer needs payment?"

They were then shown to a room where luxury was an understatement. Ermine and minx rugs, citrus wood furniture, marble and gold everything else, with large sumptuous daybeds that made soft look like a punishment. For perhaps the first time since he had stepped onto the shores of the American continent, Rufus was speechless.

What the HADES had just happened? Slaves came in and took them to private baths, where each was soaked and perfumed. So much so that at the end even Ofal no longer stunk. He seemed puzzled by this and kept waving his hand under his armpits trying to understand this unfamiliar lack of smell.

But Meridius! When she emerged she was dressed in woven gold, wearing a tiara of diamonds, and looked utterly stunning. Still as distant as ever, she wafted over, smiled gently at the Rufus and Ofal, and kissed them both on the forehead. Then her eyes rolled back in her head, and she started frothing at the mouth, making these terrible 'about to die' type of noises.

This caused an extraordinary commotion, with their host rushing in to pick her up, and take her into the anteroom, muttering "My Goddess of Light, I had no idea."

The lads follow her out and, as they come into the Ante-room, Claudius and his new best friend Garam Marsala also wander in, to see what the fuss was. "Claudius!" exclaimed Rufus. "What are YOU doing here?"

Claudius was not exactly happy to see the theatre troupe. As far as he was concerned, they had done their job, which was to help him fall on his Patrician feet in such a way as to make him rich, and now all he saw in front of him were complications.

"I say Baraka old chap, you DO realise this is the troupe that started all this nonsense that set off Focus Maximus, don't you? Do you really think it is wise to keep them around?"

Garam Marsala already had his wax tablet out and was inscribing events for tomorrow's paper. This was going to make incredible copy.

The genial host was gone. In his place, the towering presence of an African Prince stood up, and Baraka Alashad boomed out, "Fools! Have you no idea who this woman is? You complete and utter IDIOTS. Did you not realise you are in the divine presence of the Oracle of Delphi herself?"

Now, dear reader, perhaps you do not realise what this means. If you could imagine that the Pope, the President of the United States and the Howard Hughes were all rolled into one person, then this would still not make up the importance of the Oracle of Delphi. She was the one Soul that all bowed before. No nation made any decision, took any action, or confirmed any new ruler without first going to the Oracle to hear her pronouncement.

The fact that she had been missing for months had paralysed the old country. No decisions could be made, nothing could get done, and governments back there were utterly confused as to what to do about it.

Finally, she has turned up, and Baraka, her most faithful devotee had found her. "You barbarians!" He shouted at them all. "You had the wisest, most powerful being in the universe with you, and you had absolutely no idea."

"Well, to be fair," says Rufus, "We DID realise she was special, we just thought it was special in a Special Ed sort of way. The Delphic Oracle you say? Well, who would have thought it? We found her wandering about the back roads of Corinth when we were there doing some shows. We asked her name, and she said, Meridius."

"Bird Brains!" snapped back Baraka, "She IS the meridian, the OMPHALOS, the centre of the universe. And you had her in the back of a CART and had her ROWING in boats!" He weeps openly at how she had been disgraced. Meridius, AKA Delphic Oracle, then sits up in his arms, coming back to herself.

"Actually, I was thoroughly enjoying myself for the first time in my life. No cares, no worries, none of the endless parades of problems from governments to solve. But for now, we have a different problem, there is a large contingent of armed men coming here to kill Focus Maximus. Bring him to me, and Baraka, please stop all this worshipping nonsense. It is everything I wanted to get away from."

"Yes my lady," he says, bowing low, worshiping her as he grovelled out of the room.

Focus Maximus is brought in, bowing and scraping, and apologising for all the trouble. "My lady," he says in as humble a voice as he can muster, "I was going to reject the rubber chicken, but when I realised it was you, I understood you wished the augury to be performed. And it worked, but it worked terribly, horribly. I saw Rome collapsing, her institutions failing, and despair and anguish filling the streets!"

"Just like every stock market crash," she answered.

"No, worse! Even the price of housing fell!!" he exclaimed in the 'I am very worried' warbling sort of voice that Auguries have mastered.

Meridius, or whatever her real name was, the 'Oracle' sounded far too pretentious to Rufus, took Focus by the hand, gently, and said, "It is meant to be Focus Maximus, I have foreseen it. It was why I left Delphi and came here to the New World of America. The time of sacrifice is over."

The Augury looks confused, "But WHY Oracle, WHY? It has worked so well for so long, why should we change things?"

"The time is done, that is all. Do you 'really' think the Gods need the shedding of someone's blood to be appeased? I am sure the animals don't think so and, as you proved, the rubber chicken worked perfectly well."

Baraka Alashad was on one level happy that the Oracle had been found, and that she was safe, while on another level even happier that she was going to sustain the prediction, which meant all his plans to make pots of Denarii were still good. Then he realised that if she WERE right, maybe the market would NOT come back?

He walked back into the room, "Oracle, I am confused. If you wished to make the declaration of the ending of sacrifices, why could you not have done it at Delphi?"

"You mean the place full of priests and doctors? The ones with the greatest vested interest in making sure nothing ever changes? How long do you think it would have been before I had a few too many sulphurous fumes stuffed up my nose and a new Oracle was appointed? But that is beside the point, I had a vision, I saw in this vision that I must go to the New World, here to New Rome, and then the change would come of its own accord.

"And we have Claudius here to thank for it!" she says. (they all turn to glare at Claudius) "He was right in insisting we had to do SOMETHING, just having no sacrifice was not enough. This is when I realised that the Christians had the right idea."

Garam Marsala is shocked, "What the Hades? You are saying Christians have any sort of clue about anything? Those dopes insist on being fed to lions and have done so for thousands of years. How could anyone get any idea that was any good from them?"

Meridius smiled, "Because they SUBSTITUTED the sacrifice of a sheep for a pretend human. You see, they swap ordinary bread for this 'Jesus' person who they say they are eating. And they use substitute wine in place of his blood they are drinking. Obviously, they didn't quite figure on how badly ritual cannibalism was going to go down with the general populace, but when thinking of them it hit me: The Rubber Chicken prop, that would do the trick. And it DID!

"People, it really doesn't matter HOW you go about getting the augury. You could throw turnips into the air and decide the future based on what direction they land in. You don't NEED to kill anything to get a good read, you just need a decent prop!" Meridius, the Oracle, concluded.

The hard-nosed reporter was not convinced. Claudius was not convinced, Baraka Alashad was not convinced. Even Rufus and Ofal, who didn't like having to pay for sacrificial animals all the time were not exactly convinced.

Garam Marsala was the one who spoke, "Honestly, next you will be saying that LEECHES are not essential tools for the doctor!" he snorted.

However, at this point reality starting battering down the door. Over a hundred assassins and one extremely drunk Brutus were standing there gazing in looking for the Head Augury of New Rome. "There he is men! Focus Maximus, and hey, my friends! Hi Guys!" he waves at Rufus, Meridius and Ofal , though he is confused because somehow they were now clean and well dressed.

Baraka's staff suddenly turn up with clubs, to beat back the interlopers, who in turn pull out their clubs, and the mêlée begins. "Quick," says Baraka, "out the back to the chariots!"

Una Salus Victis Nullam Sperare Salutem – (Latin – written 19 BC)

The only hope for the doomed, is no hope at all...

Virgil

The Pursuit

R ufus looked at the chariot all ready to go, and he guessed the next scene. "Oh by the GODS," he said to himself, "Not a chase scene!"

But there was no time to remonstrate how much he hated fleeing from people who wanted to kill him, because there were all these people wanting to kill him. Instead, he bundled Ofal, Meridius and Focus Maximus onto a chariot and they were off.

Clattering down the cobblestones, flying along as they watched any would-be causalities leaping to one side, he chanced to look back, and sure enough, the drunk assassins were hot on their heels in some of the other chariots that had been in the back yard.

Shouting over to Baraka, he said, "We have to get to Jupiter Optimax. Do you know the way? "

"Of course," he shouted back. "But why the Hades are we going there?"

"He is the one who put the hit on Focus and he is the only one who can call it off," Rufus shouted over the noise of the metal-shod wheels.

Sparks were being thrown up as they slid around corners, with roars of anger from the chariots in hot pursuit behind them. But Garam, who had Claudius with him, had other ideas. "We have to get to Lord Rupus," he shouted to Claudius beside him.

"Why are you shouting?" Claudius shouted.

"Because everyone is shouting!" Garam re-shouted back.

These two were not the target, so the assassins ignored them as they broke ranks and headed into Manhattanus. They slowed down and Claudius could get some sort of understanding about what was happening.

"Look," said Garam, "our money is with the prophecy holding up, yes?" Claudius nodded in agreement. "Well, if they kill Focus Maximus the prophecy stands. If they get to safety and he escapes, the prophecy stands. But if we all die, the prophecy holds up but we make nothing. So no point hanging with that lot, yes? What 'we' do is get to the Daily Muse and make sure the hottest story of the millennia is published, which guarantees we get paid out of all this."

"What, we both get paid because of the story that the prophecy is true?" Claudius is clearly no reporter and has missed the important part of the whole show.

"No dumfuk, the REAL story which is that the Oracle is found and has been heard saying she SUPPORTS the prophecy. This will send

EVERYTHING into a tailspin, so we got to get the boss up to date and be ready to cash in."

In the background, the chattering of hooves is starting to fade from the pursuers, so the pair ease up to a trot. The light dawns on Claudius, "Oh, I get it, we have a contract, so Baraka is obliged to buy all the property when it crashes, but doesn't this all mean it is not a quick spike - That the whole show really IS over? This means there is no money to be made."

"Not so - Even if he dies with the assassins, the contract stands, and whose name will all the property be in? Who will be collecting the rent?"

"Ohhh," says Claudius, finally getting it.

"And who is going to go bankrupt spending all his gold on property in our name? Baraka is who, so we can buy ourselves out of slavery cheap, Because, even if he survives, he will need the money. This could not have worked out more perfectly." Garam was so pleased with himself he actually smiled, and then he went one step further and laughed. Together, they roll through the streets of New Rome, astonishingly pleased with this fortunate turn of events.

But the race to Jupiter Optimax was still on for Eruptus Non-Funnius, the Head Augury and Baraka Alashad, who had his new slave, Chincino, in tow. It was approximately at the time that the reporter and the talent agent were laughing with glee that Rufus finally realised he had somewhat overloaded his chariot. "I hope this doesn't mean an end to the troupe," he said wistfully.

Ofal laughed, and replied, "I am sure we will find another front girl, Rufus."

Rufus looked at him, once more understanding just how stupid his partner was. "No, we may all end up dead, that is what I was meaning."

"Actually," said Meridius, "I quite like the circus. I have decided to run away with you both."

"But but but!" spluttered Rufus as they careened around yet another corner, balefully looking back at the same time to see the encroaching assassins starting to catch up. "You already DID run away with the circus, remember?"

"Oh yeah, that's right," answered Meridius.

"Think of the headlines," said Ofal, "Eruptus Non-Funnius, starring the DEPHIC ORACLE! That will sell tickets."

"I am far more worried about the headline that reads 'Eruptus Non-Funnius - All Found Dead'." replied Rufus, feeling the garlic and beer breath of the assassins drawing closer.

There was no way they would make it. It was blocks to the residence of Jupiter Optimax and the assassins were almost on them. Baraka had slowed down and, while Chincino held the reigns, he was doing a remarkable job loading up arrows and shooting the odd pursuer, but there were too many.

Then a miracle occurred, from a side street Brutus Maximus emerged on a chariot and slammed into the lead horses of the assassins, blocking the street and causing utter carnage.

He leapt from the ruins of his chariot, brandishing a sword, and proceeded to chop them all down as they tried to get past. "Sorry!" He shouted as they made their way into the distance, "I thought they were here to help SAVE my uncle, not kill him!!"

Rufus shook his head. There were some forms of stupid that would never be cured, "Even with the very best leeches," he said to no one in particular, "nothing would improve that brain."

He gets every vote who combines the useful with
the pleasant, and who, at the same time he
pleases the reader, also instructs him.
Horace

Back at the Muse

Lord Rufus was astonished. This was turning out to be one of the best stories ever. "The Delphic Oracle, found? She supports the prophecy? Well done Garam, my newest lead reporter. We need to hold the presses for the changed headline. Oracle Found! Predicts the END of ROME!"

He broke out the good booze and the crystal glasses. "Drink up chaps, this is really going to stick it up Trumpetus. He's going to be caught hopping on the left foot."

"I thought he was right-wing?" Claudius said.

"He is certainly bird-brained," Lord Rufus responded.

Out rolled the papyrus team. This consisted of a thousand scribes, all called in for the scoop and now hard at work at their desks, whitening out the original headline and the entire first paragraph, to insert the new calligraphy. "Smart move getting here so fast, Garam. We have the head's up on everyone, and I have already liquidated all my stock and real estate earlier today.

"Trumpetus had the notion that the news would drive people from Real Estate into the stock market, but this information about the Oracle herself declaring the end will crash the lot all at the same time." Then he paused, looking at them, "She DID say that, yes? It's a quote?"

Garam kicked Claudius, "Sure thing, Boss. She supported Focus Maximus the WHOLE WAY." Lord Rupus didn't get to where he was without being both suspicious and paranoid over everything.

"You mean she predicted the fall of Rome, she said that specifically?"

"In as many words," said Garam. "She agreed with the head augury. She said that sacrifices had to end, she even said that they were out to kill her in the old country, which is why she came here in disguise. She even talked about ritual cannibalism and the damn Christians!"

Lord Rupus looks at Claudius, who nods, saying, "Yes boss, she said all of that. I was there and can confirm."

The owner of the New Rome Times broke out into a huge smile. "Well dammit if we don't have papers to run with for a WEEK on this!" Then he turns to some secretary who was busy sharpening a quill, "I need to get a pigeon to the Londinium offices. The Muse of the World will need this story, headline: DEPHIC ORACLE DOESN'T LIKE CHRISTIANS EITHER! That will go over big there.

The Home of Flavius Corpus

Meridius, all dressed up to the nines as she was, certainly did not look like the waif they had found outside Corinth. Tall and proud, she walked through the doorway of the Junior Consul of New Rome as if she owned the place.

And, in truth, the treasury at Delphi probably did. It was, in effect, the world bank and it held the gold deposits of just about everyone, including Baraka Alashad. She stepped through with Focus Maximus and sneered as she saw the prone form of Jupiter Optimax, who was welcoming her by abasing himself on the ground and whimpering like a beaten dog.

"If it true you put a hit on Focus here?" she asked.

"Weeeel, not quite in that sort of way ... I was merely protecting the interests of New Rome my dearest most treasured Oracle. And may I say how happy I am you have been found." he begged and beseeched and be-grovelled.

"I knew where I was the whole time," she snaps back. "Now, the reason we are here, specifically, is because you need to revoke your hit on my good friend here, don't you agree?"

"Of course, Oracle. Anything you say, Oracle." Flavius was sweating profusely, perceiving he had just given away five talents of gold for no good reason.

"Five talents of Gold? My dear friend Rufus here said this is what you offered. Seriously, you were willing to pay five talents of Gold?" The Oracle demanded to know.

"Well, yes ... that was what they asked for, him being such an important personage and all." he whimpered.

"And in doing this, you put myself and my peeps at risk, didn't you?" Meridius points out.

"Well, not intentionally, it was purely happenstance." Flavius was still face to the floor as he tried to excuse himself.

"Stand up man!" Meridius demanded. Then, looking him in his downcast eyes, she said, "So, therefore, there is a fine to pay and there's no going to the Temple of Moneta to melt down some of the statues to cover it, OR the Five Talents, you understand?" (he nods, looking deeply shocked - his OWN money?) "I seem to recall you had twenty-five talents of gold and eighty-seven talents of silver in Delphi, yes?"

Who would have thought the Oracle had such a good brain for numbers, but of course, her predecessors invented Numerology, so we should expect it.

Flavius was numb and merely nodded in the affirmative. "Very well, that should cover the insult to my person and give my troupe here a decent country property."

"It will buy them a HUNDRED country properties AND a high rise Insula here in New Rome!" he protested, but quickly grew silent. It had begun to dawn on him that the punishment for trying to kill the Head Augury made a mere death sentence an entirely pleasurable experience. "Of course, my dearest and wisest Oracle. Whatever you say."

Just as he said this, Brutus, still fighting back the assassins, had reached the steps of the house of Flavius Corpus. "Good, now go out and tell them that the hit is cancelled, but that they will all still be paid, you got that?" Meridius said.

Bowing low, he went to do exactly this. The fighting ceased, the murmuring began. Muttering unhappily about not enough people dying, the crowd of assassins departs, leaving only Brutus Maximus, bloodied but unbeaten, shouting out, "Well, wasn't THAT fun!"

Focus Maximus came out to see his nephew and, smiling, brought him inside to be cleaned up. To this day Brutus remains entirely unaware that he was travelling with the Delphic Oracle and when, some days after the events described herein, someone read him the news she had been found at Baraka Alashad's house (as he couldn't read) he said, "What a remarkable coincidence, I was in that neck of woods at the same time. Had a terrific fight!"

Needless to say, he was reconciled with his Uncle but was soon sent back to Canadia anyway because the old man liked his peace and quiet.

Captive Greece took captive her savage conquerer
and brought the arts to rustic Latium

Horace

Meeting in the Wood

Trumpetus had lost a fortune, but for every tide that changes there is a wind that blows your way, as he used to say. Mixing metaphors is an art, but sadly, one he never mastered. However, it didn't matter because he always took the confused look he left on people's faces as a sign of worship. And the priest had that same exact worshipful look on HIS face right at this minute.

"They say you lot cornered the fake sacrifice gig years ago, correct?" He hated these backwoods areas, but as this was where the Christians hung out, this was where the new money was to be made.

The priest nodded, sadly. "All gone now. Stolen, all our concepts. Everyone is doing fake sacrifices now-a-days and business has died."

"Nothing personal, but you didn't protect your interests." Trumpetus was not particularly interested in the old man's woes.

"Easy for you to say, but we were very busy avoiding lions."

"The point is, we can do a deal. I love doing deals, and you do too. And this deal we are going to do is a doosey of a deal, yeah? No need to say anything, just listen before you agree. What we are going to do is build up the fact that you all got there first, yeah? Then what we do is get you out of this bad fashion, and into ROBES. People love robes. But we are not stopping there, we are going put on a show.

"I am talking all the bells and whistles, literally bells, lots of them, and they are going to be in a HUGE steeple. And we have to build you up to be something BIG, really big, bigger than big. We are going to start painting you guys as Gods SOLE AUTHORITY because you got there first. Therefore the Gods favour YOU! You like it?" Trumpetus laid out the basics of his plan, the creation of new tax havens that he would call a religion.

"GOD favours us," the priest corrected. "Not the Gods."

"Yeah yeah, whatever rocks your boat. The point is I got connections, and I can set you up in mid-city property, so you can get out of these damp woods and set up churches inside the CBD. There you can do your non-sacrifice sacrifice thing that is all the rage, and soon you will be rolling in moola." Trumpetus cracked an amphora of Cola and drank to his own genius.

"We are not in this for the money!" protested the Priest.

"Good, then I will keep it all, and you get the converts, deal?"

"Church in town, you say, no more being fed to the lions?"

"Absolutely, and there will be gold everything, and purple robes."

"Mmmm, purple...." dreamed the priest, falling for the sin of avarice.

Aftermath

The price of real estate plummeted, as predicted, the stock market crashed and all over the world a great financial crisis was brought about by a rubber chicken. Sadly, the end of the need to sacrifice creatures shattered the lives of everyone in the augury business.

But, as the Delphic Oracle had expressly said it was OK, it was. More to the point, there was no court higher than her to argue the matter. Yes, some kept the practice up, but like smoking in public places, the whole thing became unfashionable after a decade or so.

Rome survived, but in a new form. Men started wearing beards with man-buns, and they pretended to act like they cared when their girlfriends said they were upset. Mothers even stopped beating their children with sticks when they didn't work hard enough at the local Nike Factory, and just starved them instead.

Chincino started a side business, he now worked conveyancing for Baraka Alashad and whoever else needed his assistance with the now raging property market. The ending of blood sacrifice had another side effect, it created a fairer and more humane society.

As a result, Chincino opened up offices and made a killing selling legal advice to men who now had to divorce their wives rather than just kill them when they wanted a new one. Chincino then used the money he made to set up a Multi-Level Marketing company called Rome-Way. It was advertised as, "How to lose your friends and influence nobody".

And up in Canada, they were more than happy to have the Delphic Oracle and her un-funny comedians. Speaking of which, when their three-month gig at the Quebec Coliseum finally came to a close, Rufus and Ofal were lazing about the inn, still enjoying free board and lodging, despite the fact they were now rolling in filthy Lucre.

The money from Flavius had been deposited into a new account at Delphi under the name of Eruptus Non-Funnius, which meant they were all rich. Meridius was now the star of the show, needless to say, but none of the boys minded playing second fiddle and the Canadians loved them with an enthusiasm that knew no bounds. This included girls that were throwing themselves at Rufus and Ofal. It was a pretty good arrangement.

Speaking of the Oracle, she had just walked in from an afternoon stroll amongst the adoring throngs, posing with a bicycle for the paparazzi who were out chiseling images they hoped to sell to Lord Rupus.

This was when she said, "You know, it's about time we started sorting out this Leech nonsense."

"Oh by by all the Gods - NOOOOO!" Rufus and Ofal cried.

ROME TOO
COPYRIGHT 2020 Ecallaw Leachim

ISBN: 978-0-6484277-1-1

COPYRIGHT 2020 Ecallaw Leachim
Publisher: Ladder to the Moon Productions
Email: qrcaustralia gmail.com
Web: laddertothemoon.com.au

Next comes Rome Tree!

We discover who Brutus really is, and why unicorns are banned at race tracks. A quick visit to Hades confirms how undesirable werewolves are, while a few Gods drop in to say hello, drink beer, and generally create mayhem.

Other Books from Ladder to the Moon

You will find a marvellous collection ranging from non-fiction, science fiction to modern myth at Ladder to the Moon. The two books below read like complete fiction, yet one is an biography and one is an allegory of experiences and based on real life.

Go to the website to see more. **laddertothemoon.com.au**

PSYCHIC NAZI HUNTER.

Psychic Nazi Hunter. *Very popular on Amazon. This is a remarkable biography about Alan Wood-Thomas, a well respected artist, friend of Kerouac and Ginsberg, and a man the Attorney General of the US would call in to have coffee with.*

Yet out of hours, Alan would have lucid dreams, visions of where Nazi's were hiding after the war. He would sketch their faces, write down the address he saw, and send this to friends in the French Underground. They would check and verify if the person was indeed a Nazi that went unpunished, and they would execute the individual.

Hello Planet Earth: *This will be one of the most delightful books you will ever read. In a series of short stories, the author gives an insight into just about everyone you have ever known.*

It is written as a 'Modern Myth' in that it is set in the present time, yet it is also written like an old time fairy story, or myth.

Written in 1988, when the author was in serious ill health, and not likely to survive, it has only just been edited and published. It cannot be recommended more highly.

All books available through Amazon or

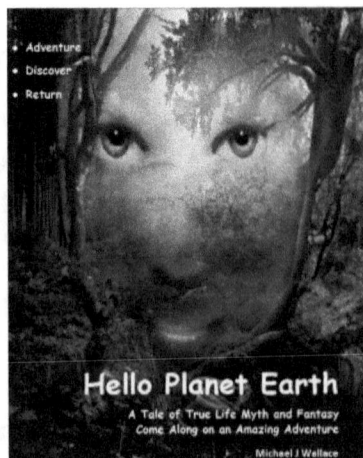

Hello Planet Earth
A Tale of True Life Myth and Fantasy
Come Along on an Amazing Adventure
Michael J Wallace

The Book of Number Series

Available on Amazon

Have you ever felt that there was something more?

The ancient art of Divination by Number is an extraordinary study you may wish to contemplate. The author of this book has written a complete course on "how to do" Pythagorean Numerology. In just WEEKS you can learn to discover and understand all the numerical secrets of the Ancient Greeks.

The Book of Number is a series of three books that cover the whole teaching of Number Divination as taught by the Ancient Pythagoreans. They are available on Amazon or direct from the author. Details are below if you wish to know more.

www.laddertothemoon.com.au

For further enquiries and updates go to the official web page at laddertothemoon.com.au.

You may also write to qrcaustralia@gmail.com.

Or go to numberharmonics.org - Here you will find all current information on Pythagorean Numerology, as well as where you can find study groups, on line classes and areas of interest to the subject.

The Dream Electric

Earth is renewed by nano-tech married to A.I. It seems like an incredible breakthrough in science, yet the little critters have their own mind own what to do!

Available on Amazon or through laddertothemoon.com.au

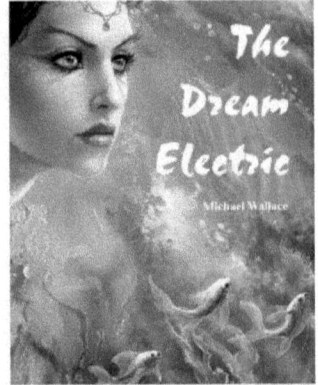

The Boringbar War

A remarkable saga of a Supreme Court, Divorce, Incest, Lies and Deceit that was written in just THREE DAYS by the Author. Based on actual events, names have been changed to protect the guilty.

Available on Amazon or through laddertothemoon.com.au

The Boringbar War

Being a Tale of the War and the Pieces Left Behind

RATOLOGY: Books I and II

Writing into a newsgroup embroiled in constant and heated argument way back at the dawn of the web, Michael diffused the anger with wisdom from the Great Rat. People kept telling the author he should record his truth-filled yet ironic statements of the obvious as a book. He went one step further, and turned them into the worlds FIRST GENUINELY ARTIFICIAL RELIGION.

Available on Amazon or through laddertothemoon.com.au

RATOLOGY
Way of the Un-Dammed
Allow Your Inner Rat to Reveal Itself!
Set Your Heart Free ... from YOU

WHO GIVES A RATS
An Expose Into the Nature of Being

The End of Times Trilogy:
Available on Amazon or at laddertothemoon.com.au

Book One in this series is called "Eat Your Fill"
Available on Amazon ISBN 978-0-9941798-3-8

This book is the first in the "End of Times" Trilogy and starts with the collapse of the entire world due to atomic annihilation.

The Apocalypse is a very interesting place, one that brings together rednecks with mutants, aliens with psychics, bikers with the mafia, and the US finally gets to elect their first cannibal as President.

Book Two in this series is called "Eat Your Religion"
Available on Amazon ISBN: 978-0-9941798-4-5

Doctor Magnusson, sent on a mad quest for ancient artefacts by the chair of the Archaeology Department at Cambridge, discovers far more than he bargained for. Time Travel, Egyptian Pharaohs, Elves and of course, the ALIENS who are wanting to take over the world.

The stakes are high. Fail and the Earth is lost to an invading army bent on destruction. And at any time, the time winds may pick him up, and throw him into the distant past!

Book Three in the Series is called "Eat Your God"
Available on Amazon   ISBN 978-0-9941798-7-6

Can you Imagine that there is a force that permeates all reality? Could you dream of a force that CREATED reality as we know it? Imagine then, if you can, that this force can also change or alter any aspect of this physical universe.

The Super Light Speed particle we call the Tachyon possesses these remarkable properties. It is the core element we must utilise in achieving Interstellar. The Brotherhood must find a way to harness this miraculous energy, and use it to send mankind to the stars.

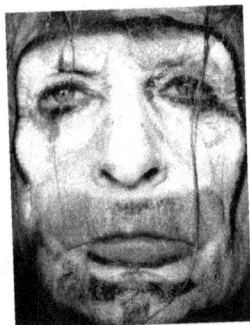

Did you like ROME TOO? Book Two in the series is already published

ROME TREE - Extract

"Were you just chatting to a bird?" Rufus asked.

"A Raven, yes. It had a message for me."

"So you understand Raven, and the Raven understands Latin? And you just happened to meet on the back road to Bethel, on your way to a horse race? Doesn't that seem like a very large and strange sort of coincidence?" Rufus is suspecting there is more to this fellow than meets the eye. "And THEN you asked it to give a cryptic message to a guy named Mars?"

"Exactly." The old man agreed and said nothing more.

A dry silence ensues for a few miles, punctuated by Ofal snoring, Meridius giggling, and Brutus muttering. The sun was beginning to hang low in the sky when Rufus remembered it would be a night of the full moon, so Rufus joked, "You don't happen to be a werewolf, by any chance?"

"No," the old man answers. "They were all banned to the underworld ages ago."

"I am very glad of that. Good executive decision by the Gods. I would hate to turn around on any random full moon and find the glowering red eyes of a werewolf staring at me like I was supper," Rufus jests.

"I didn't realise you spoke Raven," the old man comments.

"Why would you think I spoke Raven?" Rufus asks.

"Well, he was the one talking about werewolves."

"Oh, so I guess you then told the Raven to tell Mars, the God of War, to leave them where they were? And I suppose that, as one of the benefits of being a God is that you can talk with Ravens, which means you are a relative of Mars?" Rufus was starting to suspect he had picked up a seriously deranged nutter.

"His father, actually." the old man says. "Odd, you don't seem to be very scared. Most humans are scared when I am around."

Rufus laughs. Nutters he has no problem with. It is the sane ones who think they are the proprietors of truth and tradition, like Leech believers, who are the dangerous ones. "Well, we already have the Oracle of Delphi here, so why not toss in a few Gods. I am good with that!"

"Really?" he then looks at the sleeping woman. "Why, so you DO! Meridius, wake up darling, it's Zeus!"

AVAILABLE on AMAZON

About the Author

Ecallaw Leachim is considered by many to be a polymath. He is accomplished in many diverse fields, as a Master Musician, Master Body Worker, Master Numerologist, Dice Master, Recording Artist, Songwriter, and Publisher. On top of all this he is also a prolific writer with over seventeen titles in print.

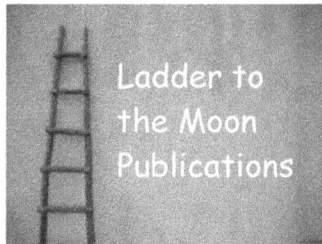

Ladder to the Moon Publications

www.laddertothemoon.com.au

Aiming for the Stars is much easier if we stop off at the Moon. We are then out of the atmosphere of our past, and can see things more clearly. We are lighter, can jump higher and further than ever before, and it takes far less energy to start each journey.

The hard part is climbing that Ladder to the Moon.

Audaces fortuna iuvat (latin)– Fortune favors the bold.

Virgil

www.ingramcontent.com/pod-product-compliance
Lightning Source LLC
Chambersburg PA
CBHW060348050426
42449CB00011B/2875